A Touch of Joy

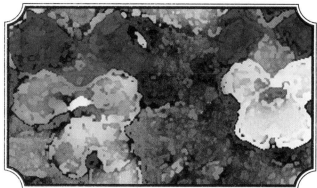

*Devotional thoughts
for women by women*

ROSE OTIS, EDITOR

REVIEW AND HERALD® PUBLISHING ASSOCIATION
HAGERSTOWN, MD 21740

The readings in this book have been selected from the three women's devotionals *Among Friends, The Listening Heart,* and *A Gift of Love.* The editor wishes to thank the authors for their contributions.

Scripture quotations marked NASB are from the *New American Standard Bible,* © The Lockman Foundation 1960, 1962, 1963, 1968, 1971, 1972, 1973, 1975, 1977.

Texts credited to NIV are from the *Holy Bible, New International Version.* Copyright © 1973, 1978, International Bible Society. Used by permission of Zondervan Bible Publishers.

Texts credited to NKJV are from The New King James Version. Copyright © 1979, 1980, 1982, Thomas Nelson, Inc., Publishers.

Bible texts credited to RSV are from the Revised Standard Version of the Bible, copyrighted 1946, 1952 © 1971, 1973.

Bible texts credited to TEV are from the *Good News Bible*—Old Testament: Copyright © American Bible Society 1976; New Testament: Copyright © American Bible Society 1966, 1971, 1976.

Bible texts credited to NRSV are from the New Revised Standard Version of the Bible, copyright © 1989 by the Division of Christian Education of the National Council of the Churches of Christ in the U.S.A. Used by permission.

This book was
Compiled by Merri Long
R&H coordinating editor: Gerald Wheeler
Designed by Patricia S. Wegh
Typeset: Garamond 14/16

PRINTED IN U.S.A.

02   5 4 3

R&H Cataloging Service
A touch of joy. Edited by Rose
Otis. Compiled by Merri Long.

1. Women—Prayer-books and
devotions.   I. Otis, Rose Marie Niesen.
II. Long, Merri, compiler.

242.2

ISBN 0-8280-0980-5

A Never-ending Task

*But he knows the way that I take; when he has tested
me, I will come forth as gold. Job 23:10, NIV.*

While enjoying a rare, quiet day at home I turned
on the television to a program that was offering
helpful hints to homemakers. The advice that
caught my attention concerned a homemade solution for cleaning
brass. The host instructed the television audience to make this solution, in an amount proportionate to the size of the pieces needing to
be cleaned, using a ratio of one cup of water to a teaspoon of both
salt and vinegar. I watched her polish to a fine sheen the items she'd
been soaking in this mixture. Her recipe seemed to work like magic!

Over the years I have accumulated several silver-plated serving
pieces and miscellaneous brass items, including a brass headboard.
I admire these things, but they continue to cost me precious time. In
order to be beautiful, each piece must undergo repetitious polishing.
Cleaning the bed is the most time-consuming, but because it looks
so beautiful when I'm done I continue to repeat the process when it
begins to look tarnished.

While preparing to entertain guests recently, I got out a couple
silver-plated serving trays. Even though they'd had a recent cleaning,
they wouldn't pass scrutiny on the buffet table.

I considered arranging some leafy lettuce around the edge of the
salad tray, but decided against it. I was sure that as the guests helped
themselves to the food the tarnish would become obvious. I was
frustrated with the frequency that these trays needed polishing in
order to be useful. I didn't have time to spend polishing tarnished
metal. I put the trays away and used glass.

As I continued to prepare the meal I reflected on a spiritual par-
allel to my decision. I was reminded that just like my silver and brass,
I too require an ongoing polishing if there is to be real beauty in my
character. Without God's frequent polishing it would be impossible
for me to "shine" for Him. However, there is a major difference between my attitude and God's concerning the polishing process.
While the frequent need to polish my things frustrates me, the Master

Designer finds joy in "polishing" the characters of His children. Praise God, He never grows weary of this process.

I can't begin to comprehend God's patience, because the only gauge I have with which to measure is the yardstick of my own human experience. But I remind myself that my heavenly Father has promised to be present in my life moment by moment. "I will never leave you nor forsake you" (Joshua 1:5, NIV). His omnipresence is one of the greatest sources of peace in the Christian life.

Today I want to be more conscious of my heavenly Father's tender concern for the polishing process necessary in my life. I want to invite Him to continue this process until I am ready to meet Him face-to-face. I want to be more like Him.   *Rose Otis*

A Good Measure for Me

Give, and it will be given to you. A good measure, pressed down, shaken together and running over, will be poured into your lap. Luke 6:38, NIV.

I was working my way through college during World War II. I was a new Christian, barred from my home because of my new beliefs. All the money I earned in my job went toward my tuition and dormitory fees, except $3 a month to cover my personal needs. I was very careful with that money.

One of the requirements at the college was that female students wear stockings everywhere on campus. Bare-legged indignity, even in the steamiest of Michigan summers, was not to be tolerated, on pain of a $1 fine. Rayon hose, costing an unbelievable $1 a pair, had replaced the newly minted nylon hosiery when they went out of production because of the war and into filmy parachutes "for the boys."

With a little mending gadget available at the time, most of us had painstakingly closed up the "ladders" in our last pair of nylons. Finally, when they became too fragile to be mended further, we had been forced to wear our rayon stockings.

*For ye shall go out with joy,
and be led forth with peace...*

Isa. 55:12

I was faithfully wearing and washing nightly my one and only pair of these less dainty hose, careful not to risk my last dollar, when the Week of Sacrifice at church rolled around. Serious about entering into all church programs, I was sad to discover I had nothing to sacrifice for the offering promoted in the nightly worship.

It struck me that sacrifice did not mean giving up something one didn't want or could do without; it meant giving up something one needed. I would sacrifice $1, Lord sparing my hose.

It had been a stressful week of late-night study and lack of sleep. I had given up my bed to my roommate's mother, who was visiting for a week. As I walked to church I realized that my venerable, much-washed rayon stockings had developed a run. Now what was I to do? The run in my stocking was devastating, and I cried as I entered the church. But when the offering plate came by I gave the $1 that I had pledged.

That evening I sewed up the run in the obligatory stockings into a clumsy seam, not to be confused with the normal seam in the back, featured on all stockings in those days. The next day I hurried from work to the dorm to bid goodbye to Ruth's mother. I was too late; she had already left. A thin box was on my bed with a note from Ruth's mother on top—a thank-you for the sacrifice of my bed. Inside the box? A pair of nylon stockings.

Jeanne Jordan

What Do Angels Look Like?

What are the angels, then? They are spirits who serve God and are sent by him to help those who are to receive salvation. Heb. 1:14, TEV.

The car was packed, and I was just starting to pull out of the parking lot when one of my tires went flat. I had a friend in the men's dorm and I called him to come to my rescue, but unfortunately he was no mechanic. We struggled fruitlessly just trying to get the jack together.

"Don't tell me you've never changed a flat before," I said.

"All right, I won't tell you," Tom said agreeably.

"What am I going to do?" I wailed. "My parents are expecting me. I'll never make it home on time."

"Need any help?"

Startled, both Tom and I turned around. Neither of us had heard anyone approach, but there he was in all his glory—a genuine mechanic, dressed in a blue gas station uniform complete with grease stains.

"I'll say we need help," Tom said gratefully. "Can you change a tire?"

"Sure. No problem." He knelt down to examine the flat. "Where's your jack?"

The smiling man changed the tire while the two of us more or less looked on. I tried to make light conversation, but apparently he wasn't much on talking.

"I really appreciate you helping me out like this. I was on my way home for the weekend when I discovered that I had this flat, so I called Tom."

"But I don't know anything about cars, so I wasn't much help," Tom finished. "Thanks for bailing me out."

The mechanic just smiled as he tightened the lug nuts and then pushed the hubcap back into place.

"There you go," he said. "All fixed."

Tom picked up the jack, and I went to open the trunk lid. By the time I got it closed, the mechanic had vanished.

"Where did he go?" I asked Tom. "I didn't get a chance to thank him or ask him his name."

"I don't know. He just vanished." Tom looked thoughtful. "Say, you don't think he was . . . an angel, do you?"

"No," I replied. "He probably just had someplace else to be in a hurry."

"Yeah, probably."

What do angels look like? Do they wear long white robes and have wings? Or were they, like people, created in God's image?

Perhaps they're like Christians, serving as the arms and legs of God. Just as in the story of the good Samaritan, our neighbor—our "angel"—could be anyone with the courage and love to do God's work here on earth. Christ said that when we help others, we are re-

ally helping Him. Maybe instead of wondering whether angels look like people, we should be wondering if people could look a little more like angels.

Gina Lee

Chosen

In him we were also chosen. Eph. 1:11, NIV.

S wish you would reconsider," I said to my daughter, Shirley. "Think about your age. Think about your children. Tammy's in college now, and Kevin will soon be in academy."

"Mom, we've thought about it. We've talked about it. I just can't leave her there," Shirley responded.

"There" meant Honduras, where Shirley and Tammy had gone to participate in an academy mission trip during Tammy's senior year. They had volunteered to do some needed work at an orphanage. In just 10 days those students had accomplished a great deal—and my daughter, a nurse, had helped out in the orphanage, taking care of some of the sick children.

"Just imagine it, Mom," Shirley continued. "All those little ones in metal cribs, whitewashed walls, no stimulation. They are rarely held—just fed and diapered, because the people just don't have time to do much else. You have to see her, Mom. She's so tiny for her age. She needs someone to love her."

"Honey," I said, "by the time she's ready for college, you and Don will be ready to retire!"

"I know," she replied. "We've thought of that too. But Mom, if she never goes to college, she will have had a better life with us than if she stays there. We just can't leave her there."

And she didn't. Shirley and Don and the whole academy and church got involved. After several months the final adoption arrangements were made, and we became grandparents again.

Three-year-old Ana could not even walk. She looked more like an 18-month-old baby. She had an ear infection. Her body was full of parasites, and her head was full of lice. Her foot had been bro-

ken, probably from a fall. But she had the biggest, brightest eyes and the most wonderful smile you could imagine! In just one hour she worked her way into our hearts, and we too could never let her go!

Ana is 6 now, still catching up physically and developmentally. She speaks clearly—you can't stop her! And she has a constant glowing twinkle in her eyes. Leave her? Never! She's our precious granddaughter!

And that's the way God is. With all our defects, problems, and cares, He loves us. No, He will never leave us nor forsake us. "He chose us . . . before the foundation of the world. . . . He destined us for adoption as his children through Jesus Christ" (Eph. 1:4, 5, NRSV). "In him we were also chosen." *Patricia A. Habada*

I Have Plans for You

For I know the plans I have for you, says the Lord, plans for welfare and not for evil, to give you a future and a hope. Jer. 29:11, RSV.

It was one of the worst times of my life. My grandfather had died, and my husband and I made a rushed trip back to Michigan over a holiday weekend to attend the funeral. When we returned to our home in Connecticut, we learned that while we were gone the organization my husband worked for had eliminated his department as part of their budget-cutting process. In two weeks he would be unemployed. It didn't take much figuring to show us that we couldn't afford to continue living in that high-rent area on my teacher's salary alone.

We checked the usual options—he searched the job ads, and I searched for a cheaper but acceptable apartment. No doors seemed to be opening for us. We tried to refigure our budget again and again, but came up with the same result every time—a quickly dwindling savings account.

My quiet time began to take on the appearance of an interroga-

tion session. "Why, God? We want to serve You. You promised to supply our needs. Why aren't You? Are You just going to let us go broke? become homeless?" Every time I thought about our financial situation I panicked.

Then I got a letter from a former student. We had been out of touch for several years. She knew nothing of my circumstances. In her letter she mentioned that she had accepted Christ as her Saviour and had a wonderful, growing relationship with Him. She also mentioned a text that was very special to her—Jeremiah 29:11. When I looked up the text and read it, it was as though God was speaking directly to me, answering all those questions I had been throwing at Him over the past few weeks. "I know the plans I have for you . . . plans for welfare and not for evil, to give you a future and a hope."

God's plans for us did unfold, although not overnight. They involved some things we never expected—including a move to another state. But they also brought blessings we hadn't dared hope for—including our own home in the country. We have had to face other tough times since then, but I don't panic anymore. I know that God does have a plan, and He will let me see the next step in His own time.

Sue Hayford

Already Ready

You also must be ready, because the Son of Man will come at an hour when you do not expect him. Luke 12:40, NIV.

During our family vacation last summer we stopped at the Precious Moments Chapel near Carthage, Missouri. As the guide led us inside the chapel and enthusiastically began telling the stories behind each cherubic painting, I found myself compellingly drawn not only to the expressive faces of the little characters but also to the themes they portrayed.

Many different scenes from the Bible were illustrated, beginning with the Creation story and proceeding through the Old

Testament stories and into the New Testament parables of Jesus and the Lord's Prayer.

As we walked from one display to another I couldn't help noticing a man and his little daughter walking directly in front of me. With her hand tucked snugly into her father's, the girl was practicing her newly developed reading skills on the captions for each scene while the father patiently coached her along. I could clearly hear their conversation as we stood in front of one particular display.

The tiny figurines seemed to be involved in various activities of everyday life while in the clouds above them Jesus was returning to this earth. The caption read: "Will you be ready?"

When the little girl had finished reading those four important words, her father looked down at her and asked, "Will you?" She turned her innocent little face up to her father and without hesitation replied, "Yes. I'm already ready."

Her simple, confident reply stopped my heart. What precious childlike faith! She hadn't said "I think so" or "I hope so." She was sure of her standing with Christ!

While tourists continued to press around me, Jesus had indeed brought a little child and set her in the midst of us and said through her innocent faith, "I tell you the truth, anyone who will not receive the kingdom of God like a little child will never enter it" (Mark 10:15, NIV).

Are you ready today?   *Brenda Dickerson*

A Voice in the Night

And the Lord came, and stood, and called as at other times, Samuel, Samuel. Then Samuel answered, Speak; for thy servant heareth. 1 Sam. 3:10.

One warm fall day our 6-year-old daughter went to play in a friend's yard after school. She had taken her new school shoes off while playing, and when she was ready to start home, they were nowhere in sight. The girls helped her look, but with no success. No matter how hard she tried, she could not

remember where she had put them, and worried that a passerby had taken them.

Heidi was crying as she came in the back door. She knew there was not enough money in the budget to replace them.

"Perhaps we'd better pray about this," I said. "The Lord knows where the shoes are even if we don't." We knelt down right then and asked Him to help us. At bedtime we asked Jesus again to let us know about the shoes. Heidi went to bed, fully believing they would be found.

Everyone slept soundly that night, but at 2:00 a.m. we were awakened by a shout and the sounds of footsteps running down the hallway in the dark. "I know where my shoes are!" Heidi cried. "God called my name in the night, just as He did Samuel's. He told me to look way back under the big bush at Lynn's house. That's where they are! I saw a picture of them right there!" She was so excited. We could hardly wait until morning to see if they really were there.

At dawn we went over and looked. Sure enough, there they were, pushed way back under the bush where no one would ever have found them. We knelt down right then and thanked the Lord for showing us where her shoes were—and just in time, too, for a cold rain fell continuously the next day.

I was so thankful that our little girl remembered the story of Samuel and how God had called him with a message in the night. What a blessing we would have missed if we had not taken time together to read those precious Bible stories.

That was more than 30 years ago, but our daughter still talks about the incident to this day. She never will forget how God called her name in the night.

Darlene Burgeson

*My heart shall rejoice
in thy salvation.*

Ps. 13:5

Hold Fast

In my distress I cried unto the Lord, and he heard me.
Ps. 120:1.

While Job and his wife were leading a comfortable life, a debate was going on in heaven. Satan felt provoked by God praising Job to his face, and his cynical question "Would Job worship you for nothing?" made at least two things very clear. First, that Satan believed people to be incurably selfish, even in their relationship with God, and second, that he was convinced not only of Job's selfishness, but also that God protected Job and favored him regardless of what really went on in his heart. When Satan left the heavenly courts, he had God's permission to prove his points.

Suddenly calamity after calamity fell on Job. When the messengers had told their terrible news, Job tore his clothes, shaved his head, and worshiped God. He had been brought up to believe that all he possessed was not his own, but had come to him from God, and he could possess it only as God permitted. Job put that lesson into practice.

But what about Mrs. Job? Did she not go through the same experience as her husband? Did she not lose all her children, her servants, her position in society, her friends—everything except her husband, who was covered with boils and who smelled so bad that it was difficult for her to be around him? She certainly did, but at the time of her loss her reaction was different from her husband's.

As long as everything went well, Mrs. Job enjoyed a good relationship with God. She had raised 10 children and taught them well, but when things started to go bad, it looks like her faith disappeared as quickly as her possessions. At that moment, stripped of almost everything she treasured in life, she could see no reason to continue her relationship with God. Nothing could be gained from it. She walked down to the rubbish heap where her husband sat scraping his sores with a piece of pottery. "You are still as faithful as ever, aren't you? Why don't you curse God and die?"

Job's and Mrs. Job's test was the same, but their reaction to the

testing was different. Why? Job stood the test because of his close relationship with God. The relationship, however, did not begin when all the troubles began; on the contrary, that was the time for the relationship to stand its test. Their friendship had grown during all the good years. Mrs. Job, however, had failed to build up this kind of relationship, and in the time of trouble her incomplete faith did not sustain her trust in God.

The story of Job and his wife gives us an opportunity to consider our own relationship with God. Do we worship God because we love Him, or for what He can do for us? Could Satan rightly accuse us of worshiping God to gain the blessings we receive? Yesterday is in the past, tomorrow is still in the future, but today is ours. Ours to seek a relationship with God that is strong enough to say: "Though he slay me, yet will I trust in him" (Job 13:15).   *Birthe Kendel*

Broken Chains

For God so loved the world that he gave his one and only Son, that whoever believes in him shall not perish but have eternal life. John 3:16, NIV.

"Where are you going, Mom?" I asked as I saw her holding her Bible, ready to leave. At that time we lived in a district north of São Paulo.

"I'm going to Romao Gomes State Prison," she answered. "We've finally got permission to study the Bible with a group of prisoners."

"That's wonderful!" I said. "But isn't it dangerous? You are the only woman in the group, and once in a while rebellion breaks out among the prisoners."

"Don't worry, dear," she replied. "God will send His angel to go with me! Many people need to be set free by the Word of God." She went with two faithful brothers, week after week, month after month, for three years before moving to another city.

Years later my mother was at a special meeting of prayer, worship, and personal testimonies at Brazil College. A Christian brother

in his late 40s came to the platform to share his personal experience. He spoke with enthusiasm for the God of heaven, who had broken his chains. He had been sentenced to 50 years in prison and certainly believed he would die in a dark prison cell. Then one day he met a lady who came into the prison and told him the following words: "Because God loved the world so much . . ."

At first he could not believe in what he was hearing. *This woman doesn't know what she is talking about,* he thought. *How could God love a man like me—a criminal, a transgressor?* But those words followed him continually, like a broken record in his mind: "Because God loved the world so much . . ." Overcome by the power of God's Word, he accepted and believed, and the Lord changed his life, setting him free from his past and from 50 years in prison.

"I owe so much to that dear sister," he continued. "I'd like to hug her tightly to show how grateful I am to the Lord and to Sister Adelaide."

Then a wonderful thing happened! Mother stood up and went to the platform. They hugged each other, and tears rolled down faces in the audience, tears of joy and happiness, because a captive soul was now set free, because "God loved the world so much . . ."

Sonia Gazeta

Engravings

See, I have engraved you on the palms of my hands.
Isa. 49:16, NIV.

He was a senior, and I was a lowly freshman. He was good-looking, wrote for our school paper, and dated one of the prettiest girls in the senior class. I think he probably knew my name, because the school I attended was fairly small, but that was about the extent of our relationship. I, along with the other freshman "hopefuls," watched from afar, sighing at the "togetherness" those upper-class students' lives

seemed to exhibit. After graduation Tom married his high school sweetheart, and a few months later we heard they were expecting a baby. This was the stuff freshman dreams were made of. Then the bubble burst. Tom was drafted and sent to Vietnam. A few months later he was sent home in a flag-draped coffin, never having seen his little girl.

I was sightseeing in Washington, D.C., enjoying the Smithsonian, the monuments, and the beautiful fall day. Quite by accident I found myself at "The Wall," that black stone monument erected as a memorial to the men and women killed in Vietnam. I paused; did I know anyone who had died in Vietnam? Yes! I knew Tom. I would find his name. I was unprepared for the flood of emotions I felt as I traced his name with my finger. Unwiped tears rolled down my cheeks as I felt the terrible loss of Tom and all the other young men and women whose names were etched into that monument. How young he was. What had become of his wife and child? What was it all for?

There is Someone Else who has watched and loved through the freshman year, through the war, and through all the ages before and since. He too feels the terrible loss, and He too has a personal stake in each of our lives.

He looks down at the palms of His hands and weeps. How He longs for us to be home with Him. He can't get us out of His mind. We are engraved on His hands.

Joni Bell

Heavenly Motherhood

He will wipe every tear from their eyes. There will be no more death or mourning or crying or pain, for the old order of things has passed away. Rev. 21:4, NIV.

As soon as I found out that we were expecting our third child, I decided to let 5-year-old Bethany in on the secret. I was always very sick when I was pregnant, and we thought the children would be less worried about me if they knew that I was sick for a special reason. But I didn't want to excite them

too much. I'd had two miscarriages before Bethany and Nathan were born, and knew that pregnancy held many hazards.

"Bethany," I said, "we have something special to tell you. Mommy is pregnant, and there is a little baby growing inside her, which is why she is so sick."

"Oh, Mommy, I'm so pleased! I was praying you'd have another baby!"

"But Bethany, I want you to know that not all babies work out. Some of them die before they are born. It's very sad. We hope and pray this baby will be all right, but we'll have to wait and see."

"Never mind, Mommy," she said. "If your baby dies, then you'll be able to have a little baby in heaven when you get there. Won't that be nice?" We'd never talked about such things, but somehow children have a way of understanding God that we seem to have lost touch with.

I'd always found comfort in the thought of angels bringing babies to their mothers at the resurrection, but my thoughts had never gone much past that point. Now I found myself imagining being a mother in heaven. What bliss! But I could hardly envisage rows of pearly-white diapers hanging on a celestial washing line outside a golden mansion! The heavenly babies in my imagination didn't need diaper changes!

It would be wonderful to be a mother with boundless energy and minimal housework. There would be no teething pain, no croup and fevers to struggle with at midnight, no days feeling heavy-headed from lack of sleep, no temper tantrums, no teenage terrors, no fear of dangers—just the joy of being together in a perfect world, sharing the delights of Paradise, watching the child grow to its fullest potential, naturally and perfectly. Motherhood as it was meant to be.

We don't know all that heaven has to offer. My wildest imaginings probably seem completely inadequate compared to the reality that God has prepared for us. But I do know that God is making it a place where all our sadnesses will end and pure, eternal happiness will begin. God's love is preparing an eternity of unimaginable joys for each one of us, whatever our earthly sorrows have been.

Karen Holford

Hidden Harm

I will restore health unto thee, and I will heal thee of thy wounds, saith the Lord. Jer. 30:17.

The afternoon sun shone brightly as my children and I enjoyed an invigorating few hours at the beach. The children laughed and frolicked as they ran barefoot over the glistening sand dunes and played hide-and-seek behind clumps of sea oats. Periods of quiet working on a sand castle near the water's edge punctuated their activity. The restless waves rolled relentlessly onto the shore, filling the moat around their castle, much to their shouts of delight. Jaunty little sandpipers darted back and forth before the ebb and flow of the waves, which made interesting patterns on the dampened sands. The day was balmy, and life seemed good.

With the gentle breeze lightly tossing her curls, my youngest daughter ran lightheartedly across the sand. Suddenly, with a cry of pain, she clutched her left foot as the blood gushed forth. Some object hidden beneath the sand had cut and gouged her foot, causing a deep and penetrating wound.

Doctor's office, sutures, tetanus shot—all followed in quick succession. Thus ended our carefree day at the beach.

Hidden objects of harm! The devil is a master at placing these traps. The path ahead looks so smooth, and life is good. Plans, schemes, sand castles fill the mind with captivating thoughts. Suddenly there is a cry of pain as some object hidden in our pathway wounds us. We are hurt through no fault of our own. Perhaps it is undeserved criticism, loss of job, disappointment, or emotional pain. We are angry. Our plans are interrupted. Why did this happen to me? Why me? Self-pity begins its infection of the wound and, like the tetanus germ, can be more deadly than the wound itself.

The Master Physician has promised to bind up the wound, and His treatment includes an anti-infective shot against the infection of self-pity and blame. "Vengeance is mine; I will repay, saith the Lord" (Rom. 12:19).

Today, if you are hurting, bruised, or bleeding through no fault of

your own, I pray you will find healing and comfort from the Master Physician, who has promised, "I will heal thee of thy wounds."

Joan Minchin Neall

Blossoming Desert

The wilderness and the wasteland shall be glad. . . .
And the desert shall rejoice and blossom as the rose;
it shall blossom abundantly and rejoice,
even with joy and singing. Isa. 35:1, 2, NKJV

One summer our family drove across Nevada. What a barren stretch of wasteland it was! Long stretches of highway with nothing but cactus, sagebrush, rocks, and dirt for company. Empty, quiet, parched, deserted, and depressing. Three or four miles felt like 30 or 40.

Every once in a while we'd come across a farm that was so beautiful one would almost want to stop and just stare at it, filling up the parched eyesight. Flowers of all colors and varieties would blossom before our eyes. Fruit trees produced in abundance and our mouths watered at the picture.

Then on we would go in the barren emptiness, hungrily waiting and watching for another one of those rare bursts of color.

After several such refreshments of beauty our family got to talking about the above Bible text in which Isaiah talks about the desert blossoming. We compared it to our own lives.

So many times we feel like a barren wasteland. Maybe you are a mother, at home by choice, but stuck in the rut of routine chores and tasks: depressed at not getting the recognition and perks a worldly career might offer; feeling empty and ugly and worn-out, like your life is a desert. God promises to make you blossom like a rose.

Maybe you are a student, in the last years of your education, feeling mentally exhausted, tired of the monotony of studying and eager to get on with your career. God promises to make your life desert

I am filled with comfort,
I am exceeding joyful in all
our tribulation.

2 Cor. 7:4

blossom like a rose.

Maybe you're a single parent, doing a job you can't stand, just because it's your only source of income; feeling as though you've got no options and there's not enough of you to go around. God promises to make your life desert blossom like a rose.

We put a picture of a blossoming desert up in our house to remind us on those desert days that there will be brighter days with bursts of color when the desert will blossom into joy and singing. Maybe you'd like to do the same.   *Shonna Dalusong*

His Perfect Strength

And He said unto me, "My grace is sufficient for you,
for My strength is made perfect in weakness."
2 Cor. 12:9, NKJV.

Life broke my heart
     And wrecked my path,
          With rocks and pitfalls, too.
I sat and wept and then I asked,
"Whatever shall I do?"
A gentle whisper deep within
I had to strain to hear
Said, "Hold My hand and take a step
And don't give way to fear."

And so I stood
And, reaching out,
I felt His presence strong;
Tentatively, a step I took—
The pathway seemed so long.
The boulders huge and pitfalls deep
Were agony supreme,
But then I heard His voice again,
"Don't be afraid to lean."

I leaned on Him,
My precious Lord,
And felt my feet grow light,
And sunshine seemed to fill the sky
Where once it had been night.
My weakness is His perfect strength,
His eyes the way will guide,
And though the path be rough at times,
We'll walk it—side by side.

Alice Covey

I Touched the Hem of His Cloak

Yea, though I walk through the valley of the shadow of death, I will fear no evil: for thou art with me. Ps. 23:4.

Never in all my life did I think that I would pass through the valley of the shadow of death, and that the words of my favorite psalm would fit so well those moments of suffering.

Death always seems distant while we are alive.

In 1990 I had surgery, apparently minor, to take out my appendix. Everything went well during the operation, but because the appendix had been hot and infected, the incision broke open one week later.

Precautions were taken for the cut to heal properly, but all in vain. Twenty days later the picture changed completely. A fever took hold of me. Nothing would bring the fever down.

On the day that this happened, my husband was traveling. He was contacted and came at once.

When he arrived at the hospital, he found me very ill. He went to talk to the doctor. The physician informed him that I had little chance to live in view of the generalized infection. He was desolate,

not knowing what to do. With much anguish in his heart he went to a dark corner of the hospital and prayed to God, asking that my life be traded for his.

On my deathbed that very night I could sense that in the valley of the shadow of death Jesus, the Good Shepherd, was by my side. I could see only His clothes, and in that instant I asked Him to let me touch Him and I would be healed.

I felt the soft touch of His garment.

Peace and a feeling of relief took hold of my heart. With a tender voice He said to me, "You will not die, dear. I love you very much."

The next morning I felt completely well. The doctor reexamined me, and the miracle was verified. The medical team couldn't believe what they were seeing.

God provided the way for me to be totally cured.

I don't know if I was dreaming, but it seemed very real to me, and tears still run down my face when I remember that I touched the cloak of my beloved Shepherd.

Today, looking back, I feel that God loves me in a very special way, permitting me to live in order to share His love with my family, my friends, and my acquaintances.

Marilisa Foffa Stina

Miracle Leftovers

Therefore I say to you, whatever things you ask when you pray, believe that you receive them, and you will have them. Mark 11:24, NKJV.

It was the summer of 1931. The Great Depression had begun, and many in the little town of Healdsburg, California, had lost their jobs and were joining bread lines. In order to increase income, Mother rented rooms to several of Dad's employees and provided meals.

One evening after supper Mother and I were cleaning the kitchen. "Bertha, look at all this food left over. I misjudged tonight! Too bad we don't have one of those new refrigerators I have read

about. Why don't we take this food to the Russell family?"

As the sun was setting we packed two large baskets of food, adding cans of beans, corn, and fruit, and started down the hill. As we walked into their driveway we noticed that the Russell family was having worship. All were kneeling in prayer. We slipped politely behind a tree. As the windows were open we could hear their prayers.

Eleven-year-old Charles was pleading earnestly, "Jesus, please send us food. We are so hungry."

Mr. Russell continued, and ended by saying, ". . . and Lord, You know how hard I've tried to get work. So far I've not had to join the bread lines. But tonight we have no food. Help me to get work so we can feed these three children. We thank Thee for hearing."

Mother and I waited before going to the door. I was 15 years old at the time, but in all the years that have gone by I will never forget what happened next.

At the first knock Charles jumped up, raised his hands, gave a big clap, and shouted, "God is sending us food already!"

Mr. Russell opened the door. "It's so good to see you, Sister Sullberg and Bertha. Come in."

Charles, ignoring his father's warning looks, announced, "Our food, Dad!" My mother confirmed his confidence, explaining that we had cooked too much and maybe they wouldn't mind leftovers.

Ready for the occasion, Charles was at the table. "Let's just start right in, Dad. I'm hungry."

Mother and I walked back up the hill in silence. "'Before they call I will answer'" (Isa. 65:24). With tears in her voice Mother spoke the text softly and with confidence. I nodded in wonder.

Bertha Appleton Glanzer

To Be Like Him

Wash me, and I shall be whiter than snow. Ps. 51:7.

I had just filled my car with gas when my eye fell on the sign "Free Car Wash With a Fill-up." I decided to surprise my husband and get the car washed. I pulled around to the car wash, rolled my window down, and put the token into the slot. I pulled forward to where the machine grabs onto the car, and waited.

I am always fascinated by those giant brushes that twirl and swirl and swab and scrub with no effort on my part. So I was watching the approach of blue bristles at least a foot and a half long. The brushes hit the windshield along with a torrent of water, and in the next moment I was receiving the worst face washing of my life. The big blue brushes along the side reached in and pounded my cheek, swabbing out my ear clear down to the drum. Of course I had no idea what was happening, so I turned to look—just in time for the second set of brushes to complete the job!

Yes, I finally got the window rolled up. And as I peered out through the soapsuds running down from my eyebrows I vowed I would tell no one about this super-shower situation. But of course I went straight home and told my husband.

God tells us in Isaiah 1:16: "Wash yourselves, make yourselves clean" (NKJV). And again in Jeremiah 4:14: "O Jerusalem, wash your heart from wickedness, that you may be saved" (NKJV).

I don't know how it is with you, but I can tell you that I struggle to be like Jesus. That is my greatest desire. To be like Him. My heart is willing, but my habits hang on. I'd like to be scrubbed up and squeaky clean spiritually. But when I wash myself I'm pretty gentle. I don't seem to do what needs to be done. I understand why David asked God to do the job for him. In Psalm 51:2 he invites God to "wash me thoroughly from my iniquity, and cleanse me from my sin" (NKJV). In verse 7 he continues, "Wash me, and I shall be whiter than snow."

When we ask, that is exactly what God does. When we finally say, "Lord, will You do whatever needs to be done? I just want to be thor-

oughly clean. Use the soap. Use the brushes. Throw in a little bleach if necessary. I just want to be clean!" He will do it. In fact, Titus 3:5 tells us it is "not by works of righteousness which we have done, but according to His mercy He saved us, through the washing of regeneration and renewing of the Holy Spirit" (NKJV). That's good news. God is in the super-shower business. And it's free. He's already paid for it. He's offering free tokens. Have you picked one up lately?

Ginny Allen

My Father's Love Letters

I have loved you with an everlasting love. Jer. 31:3, RSV.

It was a devastating blow! For the second time in six years my dad lay the helpless victim of a shattered hip. After the first break, my husband and I had invited my parents, then 82 years of age, to make their home with us. They were not relegated to "their own quarters" in our home. We lived as one happy family throughout the house. Their keen sense of humor delighted us. Their enthusiasm was contagious.

Now, again, he lay on his bedroom floor in pain. The ambulance was called, and soon Dad was undergoing surgery. He got along famously, but the shock was too much for Mother. A few days later she suffered a stroke and was obliged to enter the same hospital for surgery.

Life was never again the same. Mother's arthritis soon rendered her bedfast, and Dad was now in a full-care facility, where the six months of physical therapy seemed endless. How time dragged for each of them! Only on rare occasions was either strong enough to visit the other. Talking on the telephone was not enough. Loneliness was destroying their lives. One of us would visit Dad daily while the other stayed at home with Mother.

Then Dad's first tiny love note—written on a sheet from his little three-ring notebook—was penned. "I think about you with prayers

all the time." "If I didn't love you so much I wouldn't be so lone-some." More love notes. "I keep thinking of us together in heaven. We'll be well then." "Your sweet face never grows old; it's always young and beautiful." "We'll have new names in heaven." "Lots of love. You'll have to take a rain check on the kisses." Mother saved them all.

That little red notebook is now my prize possession—filled with love letters my father wrote from the deep painful turmoil of his heart. Tears roll down my cheeks as I read.

I have another book—one that comforted Dad daily, just as his love letters comforted Mother. Dad's name is on the cover, but my heavenly Father's name is on every page. They are His love letters to me. "I will come to you" (John 14:18). "I have loved thee with an ev-erlasting love" (Jer. 31:3). "Continue ye in my love" (John 15:9). "I have graven thee upon the palms of my hands" (Isa. 49:16). "I will never leave thee, nor forsake thee" (Heb. 13:5). "Behold, I come quickly" (Rev. 22:7). "For I the Lord thy God will hold thy right hand" (Isa. 41:13). "Fear not; I will help thee" (verse 13). "Surely I come quickly" (Rev. 22:20). Filled with pathos, they express my heavenly Father's love, His longing, His intense desire to come and take me home.

Again the tears course down my cheeks—tears of love, and of hope, and of gratitude. What a wonderful heavenly Father! I can hardly wait to see His beautiful face.   *Lorraine Hudgins*

The Tale of Two Gravestones

For God so loved the world, that he gave his only begotten Son, that whosoever believeth in him should not perish, but have everlasting life. John 3:16.

The raspy breathing of baby Joel woke me from my shal-low sleep. I recognized the symptoms of croup, dragged myself wearily out of bed, and gathered Joel up in his

*Make a joyful noise unto the Lord,
all ye lands. Serve the Lord with gladness: come before his presence with singing.*

Ps. 100:1, 2

shawl. First I went to the open window and let him breathe a few breaths of the chilly night. Then downstairs to boil the kettle.

A half hour of steam, and his breathing was easier. He was sleeping, and wearily we climbed the stairs again to bed. Tucking him into his cot, I thanked God for his recovery.

On the Isle of Wight, England, is a village church in an ancient churchyard. In the heart of that cemetery, filled with mossy, time-eroded stones, I found a tragic story of a mother's struggle. A tiny grave with one headstone. Four little girls, ages 1 to 8, died within 10 days. The stone said that they all died from croup.

My vivid imagination pictured the agony of a mother watching her children die, helpless, holding them in her arms as their breathing became more labored, praying, crying, desperate, more desperate with the loss of each beautiful daughter. I could only imagine the depth of her sorrow, her despair, a heart broken four times in two handfuls of days. As I stood by that headstone, worn by 150 years of sea breezes, my own heart ached for that long-ago mother.

Finally I pulled myself away and went on to the next stone, a young woman, not even 30. Another tragedy. And then I noticed something else. This stone was a sequel to the first.

This was the grave of the young mother, with a broken heart. Three months of profound grief was all she could bear, and then she joined her four little girls under the island sod.

The tragedy seemed to be amplified because such a simple solution could have prevented such intense sorrow. A steamy kettle in the middle of the night. Maybe she didn't realize how easily she could ease the suffering of her little ones.

Today many people are tragically dying, unaware of the simple solution that could save their lives, bringing them forgiveness, acceptance, peace and comfort, hope and joy. Jesus is waiting, knocking on the door, with all the help they need. The solution is so close, so simple, but they just don't realize it.

If I had lived 150 years ago I would have wanted more than anything else to share the simple treatment for croup with a young mother. If I hadn't, I'd have felt responsible in some way for the loss of those little lives. But maybe today there are people I'll meet in need of simple remedies to save their souls for eternity. Do I feel the same urgency to help them?

Karen Holford

All Things Work Together

*And we know that in all things God works for the good
of those who love him, who have been called according
to his purpose. Rom. 8:28, NIV.*

I have always loved children. Since I was a little girl I have been associated with babies and children. At church I would "borrow" a baby to care for or play with. During my teen years I baby-sat and worked in a day-care center. In college I specialized in early childhood education, building on my natural interests and God-given talents with children. When I married I eagerly looked forward to having a family.

When Matthew, our first child, was born, it was a period of great joy. But that joy was short-lived, because a few weeks after the birth I realized something was wrong. A visit to his pediatrician confirmed our worst fears. A yet-unknown something was drastically wrong with our firstborn. His eyes could not track a penlight in a dark room.

Then began a stream of seemingly unending visits to specialists in many fields. It was like being on an emotional roller coaster. Within six months I was told that my firstborn was legally blind and mentally retarded. Somehow I remember stumbling out of the doctor's office. I was crushed. So many hopes and dreams for my child vanished that day.

Would he ever run and play like others? Would he be able to go to school? Would he date and marry? What did a blind and mentally retarded child do for a lifework?

I don't remember being as concerned with how or why it happened. I was more concerned with how I would mother a child with disabilities. Was I equipped with the specialized skills necessary to parent a child with special needs?

During my pregnancy my husband and I had prayed for this child—a three-part specific prayer: that he would love the Lord; that he would be healthy; and that he would have a temperament that I could handle. I now recognize that God answered my prayer and continues to work in Matthew's life.

Matthew, who is now a teenager, does love the Lord and has tes-

tified verbally to it. He was baptized in a special ceremony last year by his grandfather in front of the entire church family. And he is a healthy child, even though he has functional limitations. Furthermore, he has a quiet, pliable, and adaptable temperament. He is the easiest of the four boys to discipline.

The burden of caring for a child with disabilities is heavy. It isn't something that's dealt with once and then forgotten. It's something that I live with daily. Sometimes I am overwhelmed. It's comforting to be able to turn to God in prayer and ask Him to lift this burden from me.

God is good; He answered my prayer, though not the way I would have chosen. And God began preparing me for this task as a youngster with an overwhelming love for children and through special education courses.

A promise that I claim is that God will not bring upon me more than I am able to bear (see 1 Cor. 10:13). I look forward to heaven, where my firstborn son will be made perfect—along with his mother.

Carlene Will

God Said I Could

Thy word is a lamp unto my feet, and a light unto my path. Ps. 119:105.

Teaching a feisty second-grader how to carry numerals in subtraction was proving to be a larger challenge than I'd anticipated. The determined little lad insisted on taking the smaller number from the larger, regardless of which one was on top. Then his pudgy fingers would quickly smudge in an answer.

He presented his notebook to me, a slight look of defiance playing in his usually innocent brown eyes. "All done, Miss B!"

"But Joey, how many times must I tell you? You can't do it that way!" Exasperation edged my voice.

His reply was swift and sure. "But my mommy said I could!"

Ah! Such loyalty. If Mommy but says the word, it's gospel truth.

No room for misunderstanding or argument. That's just the way it is.

Joey eventually learned to carry in subtraction.

And I learned a lesson in devotion.

If only we could have such loyalty to the words of our heavenly Father. If God said it in His Word, it must be true. We can follow it unconditionally—no questions asked.

Why did I take a mighty leap in faith and accept Jesus as my Saviour? Because God said I could.

Why do I confess my sins and leave them behind me in the deepest ocean? Because God said I could.

Why do I walk in assurance each day, holding on to the hand of my Best Friend? Because God said I could.

How am I able to love my enemies? Because God said I could.

The world may ridicule us for following God's words. We may be told that we misunderstand, that what God said isn't important anymore.

But like Joey, our devotion to our heavenly Parent should be such that if God said it, we do it. We know He loves us more than any earthly parent and He tells us to do only what is for our own good.

I choose to give my life in total surrender today to the leading of the Holy Spirit. God said I could.

Dawna Beausoleil

The Saviour's Hand

And immediately Jesus stretched forth his hand, and caught him, and said unto him, O thou of little faith, wherefore didst thou doubt? And when they were come into the ship, the wind ceased. Matt. 14:31, 32.

Our daughter Amy was born with many problems. Some were visible, such as a cleft lip and palate; some were not. A couple hours after her birth the doctor discovered that she had a diaphragmatic hernia. By the time she was 16 hours old she'd been transferred to another hospital and was having her first surgery.

The hospital was an hour away from us, but every day we made the long trip to see her. In time Amy recovered from her surgery, and the hospital staff asked us to come learn how to feed her so she could eventually be released to come home.

When the happy day came, it was a surprise. I had to call home to have someone bring some clothes so that I could dress Amy for her homecoming. Her doctor asked to see us before we left. He sat at his desk and told us that Amy was trisomy 13, just a couple steps down from trisomy 21, Down's syndrome. "Her prognosis is not good," he continued. "She has a 20 percent chance of living four months, and a 2 percent chance of surviving two years. The rest of the children with her condition die by age 4 or 5," he said. Only two children had been known to live longer.

For the next several months it was like living in the midst of a storm. Amy cried most of the time. Her two weeks in the hospital had taught her that touch meant pain. If we hugged or kissed her, she cried. Feeding gave her gas, so she cried! And she didn't trust us. It took months and many hours of careful, loving care to break through.

It was easy to get so wrapped up in Amy's care that I'd forget to take time out for God. So many times I found myself sinking in a sea of despair. One terrible day it all seemed to be pulling me down. I felt like the water was closing up over my head and I was going to drown. I finally sat down and told God I couldn't do it by myself anymore. Like Peter, I reached out and took the Saviour's hand. With that a peace settled over me that I will never forget.

How often we forget the Saviour's hand is there waiting for us. All we need to do is reach out to Him. He'll never force it on us. The storm around us will not always go away. But He will always be there to get us over the rough waves and into the calm. I wish I could say that I always hold His hand, but I often let go. *But thank You, God, for always being there. You remind me of Your love every time I think of Amy. She will soon be 18 years old!* Linda Reynolds

The Lord Wore Old Clothes

Then the righteous will answer him, "Lord, when was it that we saw you hungry and gave you food, or thirsty and gave you something to drink? And when was it that we saw you a stranger and welcomed you, or naked and gave you clothing? And when was it that we saw you sick or in prison and visited you?" And the king will answer them, "Truly I tell you, just as you did it to one of the least of these who are members of my family, you did it to me." Matt. 25:37-40, NRSV.

My 41-year-old husband, Wayne, had lost his year-long battle with colon cancer. Now he was sleeping in painless peace, waiting for the Lord to come. I felt so alone. All I seemed to be able to say to the Lord was "Help me!" How was I to be both mother and father to my two children? How could I go on without my beloved husband? I remember desperately praying, "Lord, I need You now. I need Your comfort, support, and strength."

And He came. No, not in white robes. Not even in a vision. He came disguised as my neighbors, my church friends, my husband's colleagues from the Christian college at which he had been a chemistry professor for 12 years.

On the day Wayne went to the hospital for the last time, the Lord came in the form of four ladies in old clothes, who cleaned my house from top to bottom. (I hadn't done much cleaning since my husband had become ill.) They had arranged for another friend, a motherly lady who had seen a lot of sadness and knew how to listen, to take me out for a long lunch.

When we returned, these four dust-covered representatives of my Lord were gone. My house was spotless (even my 8-year-old daughter's closet!). In the main bedroom, where my husband had spent most of his last six months, the furniture was rearranged, and on the bed were brand-new sheets and a matching bedspread,

all in a colorful, happy print!

The love that reached out from them to me was overwhelming. I remember lying facedown on the bed and sobbing. Later I found a note in the kitchen telling me what had been prepared for supper. All I had to do was follow the simple directions they'd left for me.

After I became a widow, the Lord came in old jeans to move my household belongings to a smaller house, closer to the school at which I taught and the children attended. He also came bearded, in sixties' caftan, and worked in the yard, doing whatever Wayne would have done had he still been alive.

Later He stopped in after work to cut boards to the right size for bookshelves. I had thought we didn't need help, but neither I nor my 13-year-old son knew how to use the circular saw, and we were both afraid to try it.

To recount all the ways the Lord came that year would take pages. All those dear people who were His arms and His hands to me—how could I ever repay them?

It took awhile before I realized that I could repay them only by being the Lord's arms and hands to someone else in need. I didn't deserve His (and their) goodness to me, but I received it in full measure, running over.

Lord, make me aware of the pain and suffering around me, and let me be Your arms and Your hands to someone in need. Amen.

Sandy Zaugg

Bag Lady

I delight greatly in the Lord; my soul rejoices in my God.
For he has clothed me with garments of salvation and
arrayed me in a robe of righteousness. Isa. 61:10, NIV.

"Come on, get the lead out," my husband called as he pushed through the crowded street. "We need to get out of here before the evening rush hour."

Our family had packed a lot into this day of sightseeing in

Now unto him that is able to keep you from falling, and to present you faultless before the presence of his glory with exceeding joy... Jude 24

Philadelphia. So now with aching feet and weary bodies we hustled toward the car.

"A shortcut down this side street, and we'll be there."

That's when I collided with her, at least her shopping cart. The cart tipped, and things tumbled across the sidewalk.

"Oh, I'm so sorry. Let me help," I offered as I bent to right the cart.

She mumbled something, and I looked at her. Stringy, dirty hair fell across her gaunt face. Tattered, filthy clothes hung from her bony body. I was repulsed, but then—for a moment—her eyes met mine, and it was as if I looked into her soul. Despair, confusion, and hopelessness confronted me.

My heart was torn, and I wanted to reach out to her. But it happened so quickly. A heartbeat later she was gone, pushed along, lost in the crowd.

That night I could not stop thinking about her. Where was she? What would it be like living on those dark, lonely streets? Was she hungry? cold? sick?

I looked around me. I loved my home. Though it was not elegant, it was comfortable. I enjoyed sitting by our wood stove on cold nights and soaking up its warmth. I liked the way the lamplight shone on the woodwork. I enjoyed the ticking of the clock on the mantle and the soft voices of my boys upstairs as they talked about the day's events. All around me were mementos of the people and things that I cherished.

How would it feel to give it all up? to bid my family goodbye and go back out into the dark, cold night? to drive into the city? to search every alley, every street, until I found her? and when I found her, to put my arms around her and with love and compassion offer her the life that was mine in exchange for the fate that was hers? How would I feel as I placed upon her cold, frail body my warm, clean clothes and put on her filthy rags? I shuddered to think of the shame, humiliation, and death that would be mine.

As I thought of her, I thought of Someone Else—Someone who had left His heavenly home for us all. And though I cannot understand it, He would have come for just me. He searched until He found me. He encircled me with His love. He took my despair and gave me hope, took my fear and gave me peace. He covered my filthy, sin-stained garments with His pure, clean robe of righteous-

ness. He suffered the shame and death that should have been mine so that I could have the life that was His, and someday I shall live in His home for eternity.

Rebecca J. Grice

Do You Really Know Jesus?

I count all things to be loss in view of the surpassing value of knowing Christ Jesus my Lord, for whom I have suffered the loss of all things, and count them but rubbish in order that I may gain Christ, and may be found in Him, . . . that I may know Him, and the power of His resurrection. Phil. 3:8-10, NASB.

A 97-year-old lady received visits from her pastor. On one occasion she told him that when she was a little girl she had visited the White House and shook hands with President Lincoln. If someone were to ask you if you knew President Lincoln, you would probably respond, "Of course, he was the president of the United States during the Civil War and was known as Honest Abe." We don't know Abraham Lincoln like this 97-year-old lady did; and she didn't know him as did his son, Tad, who could burst into his dad's study at any time, jump up on his knee, and get a bear hug and kiss. The son really knew Abraham Lincoln, wouldn't you say?

Do I really know Jesus? is the ultimate question in life. While I was in college one of my professors, Marjorie Kemmerer, impressed me with her Christian life and influence. She had a close relationship with Christ, and this was evident to all who knew her. I discovered that her secret of knowing Him lay in the fact that even though her first class for the day began at 7:30 a.m., she would rise at 4:30 a.m. in order to have quiet time with the Lord. Jealously guarding a daily quiet time spent alone with Jesus, communing with Him through prayer and Bible study, is not an option. The only way

Jesus knew His Father while on earth was through the same avenues open to us.

E. M. Bounds states beautifully, "In prayer, God stoops to kiss man, to bless man, and to aid in everything that God can devise, or man can need." That includes everything!

Susanna Wesley, mother of 19 children, had no place to go to meet the Lord where she could be alone. At her chosen time she would take her apron and cover her face. Her children knew never to disturb their mother when she was praying in her apron!

Jesus will make Himself known to us when we pour out our souls to Him in prayers of thanksgiving, intercession, and petition. Let us thank God for the privilege of communing with Christ in prayer and Bible study, which is the way to really get to know Him as our Friend and Saviour.

Marie Spangler

The Waiting

He who testifies to these things says,
"Yes, I am coming soon." Rev. 22:20, NIV.

They stood next to the car, a bouquet of little girls, begging me not to leave. "Don't go, Mommy. Please don't go."

"When are you coming home?"

"Take me with you."

I looked helplessly at my husband, Gerald. The trip was necessary. Unavoidable. We would be gone a mere week, and my father had come miles to stay with our daughters. They would be fine. They would stop crying.

I gave each one a final hug and turned toward the car, but the 8-year-old clung to me, tears raining down her cheeks. At last I pried her arms away, trying to brush away her tears with promises of return. Time means little to a child, and she would not be comforted.

Gerald started the car. We backed up, turned, and slowly drove away while my father shepherded the girls toward the house. Noelle stopped, digging her fists into her eyes. I saw her lips move, but I

couldn't hear her words. Then I let my own tears fall, vowing that I'd never leave a child that heartbroken again.

It was nearly midnight when we arrived in Washington, D.C. In the motel room I called home, even as I kicked off my shoes. Dad said that the children were fine. They were asleep, of course. I shouldn't worry.

The days passed, the hours packed with meetings, questions, and problems. Each evening when I fell into bed, my mind traveled backward, across black ribbons of highway, down the Shenandoah Valley, across Virginia, through the Smoky Mountains and middle Tennessee to our own four acres and tree-covered ridge, my morning glories, and three little girls who counted the days until our return.

Not that they missed me every moment. I knew that, no doubt, my thoughts turned to them more often than they thought of me. Their grandfather was a good baby-sitter. He'd buy popsicles and potato chips for them, walk with them in the woods, push them in the swings. He could be persuaded to talk about the olden days and would probably let them stay up past their bedtime. Mostly I thought of Noelle. I could not erase the feel of her arms around my neck, and I knew that she especially was waiting for me to get home.

Finally the time came for the trip back. We packed our suitcases, got up early, and headed south. Traffic was light, the sun bright. It felt good to be going home.

And yet 700 miles is *700 miles,* and the 55 m.p.h. speed limit made them drag. The sun climbed, hung directly above for a short while, then began its descent, faster, faster, until lavender shadows bathed the distant hills. Then darkness. We were still a long way from home.

Somehow, with the falling darkness, I felt desolate. My children were waiting, and through no fault of my own I wasn't there with them. If sheer will could have bridged the distance, if love could have erased the miles—but it couldn't. Three little faces etched in my memory called me home. Three little children waited, and we were late.

In the darkness, the car slowly covering the miles, my mind wandered beyond this homecoming. Could it be for Christ, as for mothers throughout history, that the pain of separation is all the more intense because He knows His children are anxiously awaiting His return? Could Christ's heart possibly ache as badly as mine did then,

wanting to will the miles away, mentally clasping each landmark to my heart, so glad to be nearing home? Or does Christ have an infinite capacity for longing, for love?

Perhaps that is why we are told that "it is of the Lord's mercies that we are not consumed, because his compassions fail not" (Lam. 3:22) and "the Lord is not slack concerning his promise, as some men count slackness; but is longsuffering to us-ward, not willing that any should perish, but that all should come to repentance" (2 Peter 3:9).

Penny Estes Wheeler

The Seven Last Words of Christ

It is finished. John 19:30.

The composer took for the name—and content—of one of the most popular religious oratorios, "The Seven Last Words of Christ." He could have chosen "The Seven Last Miracles" or "The Seven Last Trips" or "The Seven Last People He Saw." But no, Theodore Dubois selected the seven last words—sentences, actually—that Jesus spoke, and in so doing gave artistic permanence to Jesus' final utterances.

Actually, anyone's dying words are valued as some of the most significant ones the person has spoken. After a death, the loved ones want to know whether a note was left, whom the person talked to last, what the person said. A soldier's last lingering comment before going off to war is indelibly etched in his family's memory. The final phrase a lover whispers before leaving is what is most treasured.

Lawyers make a living from writing up in permanent form a client's last will and testimony, being paid handsome sums to make the words legal. Law offices, high-voltage places in general, often get unusually intense when wills are read. Who will get the business? Who will get the house? Who will get the money? One rich old lady

abolished all hopes of her heirs getting wealthy when she left all but one dollar to her cat!

In Jesus' last will and testimony, His seven last sentences, whom did He remember? Were you in it? According to Dubois' Oratorio, Jesus' final words were as follows:

"Father, Father, forgive them, for they know not what they do." And Jesus remembered His tormentors.

"Verily, thou shalt be in paradise with Me. Amen, so I tell thee." And Jesus remembered a hardened criminal.

"See, O woman! Here behold thy son beloved." And Jesus remembered His mother.

"God, My Father, why hast Thou forsaken Me?" And Jesus remembered His knowledge of the terribleness of sin.

"I am athirst!" And Jesus remembered His humanity.

"Father, into Thy hands I commend My soul." And Jesus remembered His faith in God.

"It is finished!" And Jesus remembered His mission, to this earth and to all others besides.

"To the angels and the unfallen worlds the cry, 'It is finished,' had a deep significance. It was for them as well as for us that the great work of redemption had been accomplished. They with us share the fruits of Christ's victory" (*The Desire of Ages*, p. 758).

Oh, wonderful irony—Jesus' dying words became words of life for the entire universe. His death utterances gave hope of immortality. We are all in His will.

Wilma McClarty

Eyes That See

Then Elisha prayed, and said, "O Lord, I pray thee, open his eyes that he may see." 2 Kings 6:17, RSV.

When I was a young girl I didn't enjoy books, and did very poorly in school. It wasn't until I was 10 years old and in fourth grade that a teacher finally realized that I was straining to see the blackboard. She sent

me to the school nurse for a simple eye test. You know, the kind in which you stand about 20 feet from a large poster featuring letters of the alphabet, cover one eye at a time, and read the letters. When I took the test I couldn't see any letters from the second row down. The nurse sent a note home telling my parents to take me to an eye doctor. My eyesight was so poor that I was legally blind!

I'll never forget the first time I put on my new glasses and looked around. I could see things across the room! I looked out the window and could see birds flying, leaves on the trees, blades of grass, and flowers. I had never seen a bird fly before. The people walking by on the sidewalk had faces and expressions I could see. I went to school the next day and endured the taunting chants of the children calling me "four eyes," and didn't even care. I could see, and that was all that mattered. The blackboard, the teacher, the students, the bulletin board . . . everything was in focus. A whole new world opened up to me!

I was so excited. I just couldn't see enough, fast enough. I was hungry to take everything in. I have often contemplated that experience and thanked God again for the gift of sight.

Sometimes we become "out of focus." We do a delicate balancing act between our families and careers. We struggle with problems with toddlers and teenagers, communication with our husbands, trying to "keep up with the Joneses" while living within our budgets—and the list goes on and on! We look inward and allow our personal problems to blur our spiritual vision. May our daily prayer be "O Lord, keep me in focus. Help me to keep my priorities straight. Open my eyes that I might see!"

Celia Cruz

*But the fruit of the Spirit
is love, joy, peace...*

Gal. 5:22

The Power of a Song

Speak to one another with psalms, hymns and spiritual songs. Sing and make music in your heart to the Lord. Eph. 5:19, NIV.

It is common knowledge that singing brightens life and that spiritual music is able to elevate the human heart to God. Many Christians have received comfort through spiritual music, but spiritual songs can impress godless people as well. They can even banish evil, with divine assistance. I experienced this in my early youth.

It was the year 1945 at the end of World War II. I was a 16-year-old girl when the Russian Army advanced toward Vienna. Because of the bombing raids, my parents had fled with me to the countryside, where we were living in a small village near the Danube. We knew about the advance of the Russian Army, and one evening we saw Russian tanks on a nearby wooded hill. The inhabitants hoisted white flags on the roofs. Everyone wanted to escape alive and hoped that the war would soon be over.

After evening prayer we went to sleep unsuspecting of all that would happen during the night. In the morning there were violent knocks at our door. My father opened it, and Russian soldiers stormed in to thoroughly search the house for weapons, wine, and valuables. As my frightened mother saw the menacing look on the soldiers' faces, she motioned to me to play at the harmonium. With trembling hands I played the only two hymns I knew by heart, and hoped that the music would somehow impress these wild-looking fellows.

And then the miracle happened. One after the other, they left the house. Then others came in, listened for a while, and disappeared. I don't remember how many times I played these two hymns over and over, but God helped us through a time when we were unaware of our tragic situation. While we were sleeping that night, strong angels must have guarded our door, for the surrounding people suffered terribly from looting, beatings, shootings, and rapes. God had given my mother the idea that the spiritual songs could soften the rough spirits, and He literally "shut the lions' mouths," as was the case with Daniel.

Oh, that we would use the spiritual songs more often! Words and melody are meant to comfort and uplift us, and to elevate our minds toward God. Many people have had encouraging experiences with these hymns.

Susanne Hatzinger

"I Like Myself, but ..."

For we dare not make ourselves of the number, or compare ourselves with some that commend themselves: but they measuring themselves by themselves, and comparing themselves among themselves, are not wise. 2 Cor. 10:12.

The young church usher gazed into a full-length mirror, lamenting over those aspects of her reflection that were less than pleasing to her critical eye. Her thoughts turned to the church secretary, who seemed to be almost perfect. The young woman sighed and said, "I like myself, but I am too tall and thin and my hair is too curly. I wish I could be poised and elegant like the church secretary."

The church secretary paused before her full-length mirror, and her thoughts turned to the young church usher who seemed so bubbly and cheerful. "I like myself, but I am too short, and my hair is hard to manage. I wish I could be as bubbly as the church usher."

Comparisons. We compare shoe size, body measurement, and weight. We compare the ability to cook, sew, decorate, and organize a home. We compare not only our own abilities or lack thereof, but also the abilities of our husbands, children, and even our pets! We compare our worst characteristics with another's best attributes. We set ourselves up for disappointment and dissatisfaction and then exclaim, "I like myself, but . . ."

Scripture speaks very clearly about this habit we have of comparison. We are told that comparing ourselves with others is not a wise practice. Another human being is an insufficient measuring rod for beauty, accomplishment, or success. In addition, it is not wise because comparison sets up an adversarial relationship with others and

is counter-productive to spiritual as well as emotional growth and development. Comparison ignores God-given strengths while assuming another's blessings are better.

As one author stated: "We are not hen's eggs or bananas, or clothespins, to be counted off by the dozen. Down to the last detail we are all different. Everyone has his or her own fingerprints. Recognize and rejoice in that endless variety. Rejoice today in the uniqueness of yourself. Learn to enhance your God-given strengths and gifts of others and learn to say, 'I like myself because . . . !'"

Barbara Tobias

My Curse—A Fountain

*She left him and afterward shut the door behind her
and her sons. They brought the jars to her and she kept
pouring. When all the jars were full, she said to her son,
"Bring me another one." But he replied, "There is not a
jar left." Then the oil stopped flowing.*
2 Kings 4:5, 6, NIV.

Have you ever been down to your last dollar? I have. And so had the widow whose story is told in the fourth chapter of 2 Kings. A poem from *Eve's Version*, by Nova Schubert Bair,* tells the widow's story.

"WHAT DO YOU HAVE IN THE HOUSE?"

Elisha asks me. Does he not hear?
My husband has died; a creditor
stands ready to lead my two sons
away as slaves. Nothing is left
to buy their freedom—unless my favors?
I shrink from his words. "Just something
in the house," the prophet reassures.

"Only a pot of oil," I answer.

He bids me borrow vessels.

Now they are standing ready. I close the door.
My curse becomes a fountain as I pour.

Isn't that beautiful? The presumed curse became a fountain. The widow was told to sell, pay her debts, and live!

There was a time when I had not one dime left over in any week. Then someone asked me to give a weekly Bible study with a family that lived 20 miles away—40 miles round trip. My miles were measured by the cost of gasoline. Could I do the study? The Lord said that I could.

For one year I went the extra 40 miles through the city and gave the study without one penny increase in gasoline cost. It was as if there were no extra miles. The person with whom I studied that year gave his heart to the Lord, as did one of his sons. My lack of money did not prevent God from creating a fountain for hungry souls.

Elizabeth Sterndale

---

* "What Do You Have in the House?" by Nora Schubert Bair, appeared in *Eve's Version: 150 Women of the Bible Speak Through Modern Poets,* and is used by permission of the author and Paramount Publishing Company.

Be Careful

Have I not commanded you? Be strong and courageous.
Do not be terrified; do not be discouraged,
for the Lord your God will be with you wherever you go.
Joshua 1:9, NIV.

I stand, the telephone to my ear, talking to my father. It's late, and he's leaving for Texas at 6:00 a.m., planning to drive the 1,300 miles in two days. He is 78 and I worry about him.

I ask if he's finished packing. I tell him to say hello to assorted

relatives. I make him promise not to pick up hitchhikers. His voice is deep, dear, precious. I don't want to let go.

The conversation lags, but I keep him close with my questions. I want to hold on to him, to ride the long highway with him, keeping him safe and bringing him back.

"I guess I'll watch the 11:00 news and go to bed," he tells me. "OK."

A pause. "Well," he says, "see you in a couple weeks."

"OK, Daddy. You be careful."

I open her bedroom door in the predawn darkness and tiptoe across the room. She'd asked me to wake her before I left for the airport, so I bend down to touch her arm. "Goodbye, Noelle. I'm going now."

It's snowing outside, and I'm a little worried about the drive to Baltimore. She stretches, my 17-year-old daughter, and I touch her hair. "Goodbye. It's 5:45 a.m. I'm leaving."

Eyelids flutter. "'Bye, Mommy. Have a good trip."

"I will."

"Be safe."

I promise to be safe, as if I had any control over slick highways and airplane flights. This is the downside of travel. Leaving those who love me. She squeezes my hand. "Be careful."

We're putting her on a British Airways jetliner, our eldest daughter, sending her—no, *letting* her—fly across the ocean to Newbold College. She is wearing a new green coat and dark-green leather gloves. Her eyes sparkle. She loves England and the school there. She is utterly happy, and I am utterly desolate.

A voice announces that her flight is ready to board. I hug her, and she laughs. "Are you going to let go of me?"

Now I laugh. "Of course! You have a good flight." I walk with her a few more steps. One more quick squeeze. I let her go, and she gives me a smile of pure radiance.

Caught up in the crush of people, she reaches the flight attendant and hands him her ticket.

"Robyn!"

She turns for a heartbeat.

"I love you. Be careful."

I love you.
Be careful.

In our family the phrases are interchangeable. They mean the same thing. *I love you. So take good care of yourself. Be careful.*

You are precious to me. I can't bear to see you hurt. Part of my heart and soul, *you are cherished beyond words. So be careful. I love you.*

My thoughts turn to God, our all-loving Father, and to Jesus, who became one with us, forever bound to us by a human body. They know, far more than we, the hurt and harm that merely living brings to Their earth children. And so They sent us the loving message, repeated in a thousand different ways: *Be careful. I love you.*

"Be firm and brave, never be daunted or dismayed, for . . . God is with you wherever you go" (Joshua 1:9, Moffatt).

"Be careful," God pleads. For "your enemy the devil prowls about like a roaring lion looking for someone to devour" (1 Peter 5:8, NIV).

"Be wise."

Keep the laws I have given you, these 10 rules that will safeguard you against a thousand dangers. "Watch and pray so that you will not fall into temptation" (Mark 14:38, NIV).

"Be careful," God says. "I love you."   *Penny Estes Wheeler*

The Ultimate Transaction

I delight greatly in the Lord; my soul rejoices in my God.
For he has clothed me with garments of salvation and
arrayed me in a robe of righteousness. Isa. 61:10, NIV.

My mother has a unique knack for telling the most tear-jerking stories as matter-of-factly as if she were relating tomorrow's weather forecast. Her voice devoid of emotion, she relates all the galling details, then walks off into the kitchen to start the potatoes. Left gaping on the couch, my sisters and I shake our heads in disbelief, yelling after her, "But what happened next?" She rarely remembers.

One of her choicest stories, never failing to produce a scene of intense melodrama in our living room, concerns an incident that occurred when Mom was about 8 years old. The story begins with Mom—back in a day when 25 cents bought a lot more than a call at the corner phone booth—receiving two quarters from a generous relative.

The silver was tucked away and spent mentally on every conceivable joy an 8-year-old girl could imagine. But one day Mom took out the two precious quarters, dusted them off, and slipped them into her skirt pocket for a very special occasion: a carnival had come to town.

Reluctant to part with her treasure, Mom wandered happily through the fairgrounds, content just knowing that the brightly colored displays were all hers, should she want them. When it was almost time to leave, a vendor of mysterious packages began making his way through the crowd.

"Gifts from all over the world," he called out in a cunning voice. "Just 50 cents, and you can own the most beautiful things humans can imagine: dazzling rings, sparkling glassware, lovely vases . . ."

Mom's heart raced as she reached out to grab the man's coat, which seemed to be all too rapidly flapping by her. The transaction was a quick one. Two quarters. One plainly wrapped package. And then the voice, above her, booming out into the nameless crowd, "This young lady just won a beautiful watch!"

Little fingers fumbled with the prize, a small heart bumped rapidly in anticipation. And then the box was open before her, revealing its contents: an empty, broken perfume bottle. "Oh, sir," came the trembling voice, "there's been a terrible mistake. Oh, sir . . ."

But the man promising the world had disappeared into its farthest reaches.

Empty glass; an empty promise. A broken bottle and a broken dream. The exchange of a treasure for a cheap fraud. One of life's unfortunate inequities.

Sometimes it seems as if our entire existence is made up of exchanges. We exchange our singleness for a lifetime partnership. Some discover the joy of being two; others face a lifetime of emotional abuse and misery. We exchange our time for a career. And with that transaction may come creative challenge and fulfillment . . . or the feeling of being caught in a relentless machine, merciless in its demands. We exchange our money for luxuries, and so it goes, and so we live. Sometimes winning; other times, standing openmouthed,

*My breathren, count it all joy
when ye fall into divers temptations.*

James 1:2

staring into an empty, broken perfume bottle.

Christ tells us He will give us His righteousness in exchange for our filthy rags. And that is the ultimate transaction. Life can bat us around, rob us of the tangibles and the intangibles, until we feel we have nothing much left to offer. Yet Christ is still waiting, with a spotless robe of pure white. And the best part of it is, we don't even have to relinquish the two quarters.   *Sandra Doran*

Beautiful Attitudes

Blessed are those who keep my ways. Prov. 8:32, NIV.

How blessed is that woman who knows her need of God, for only then can others find a bit of heaven in her presence.

Blessed is that woman who finds in sorrow the comfort of a living God, who learns that although life is burdened with unhappiness, a heart overflowing with gratitude can seek and find such fullness of joy that all bitterness is crowded out.

Happy is the family of the woman who possesses a gentle spirit. Her husband will place his world at her feet; her children will come often to her door. She truly listens and surely hears.

How blessed is the woman who yearns for justice and does something about it—shares her home with the homeless, her food with the hungry, her joy with the desolate—yet cares for the needs of her own family, including them in the sharing.

Happy is the woman who knows how to forgive, who cannot hold a grudge, and asks others for forgiveness. Divine forgiveness shall be hers.

Happy is that woman whose heart is pure, swept clean of self-pity, nagging, and complaints. In her heart is abundant love for her husband. So happy will her marriage be that others will see God in her home. Even their children shall behold Him.

How blessed is the woman who is a peacemaker, sharing neither gossip nor faultfinding. She studies her children to learn how to

bring peace to them. She has self-esteem because God is her Father. Her children respect her because she is fair and just. She teaches them how to become members of God's family. Heavenly peace shall dwell deep within her soul.

Can this woman be happy when she has been misunderstood, mistreated, unappreciated? Yes, for she has exchanged her will for God's peace, joy, and love, and she will be given God's crowning gift—heaven! *Chesapeake Partners*

Of Lace and Love

Does a . . . bride forget her wedding dress? Jer. 2:32, TEV.

As the mother of a recent bride, I can tell you that it will never happen. From the moment Mark proposed to my daughter, Kelli, my sane little world dissolved into a maelstrom of bridal magazines, bridal patterns, bridal salons, bridal fashion shows, bridal satins and laces at the local fabric shop. On one fact mother and daughter agreed. Kelli would need a wedding gown. Neither considered anything less.

On our first day of "just browsing," Kelli found her dream dress. She tried it on. One look in the three-way floor-length mirror and she announced, "This is the dress." One glance at the price tag that read $2,300 and I announced, "Not on your life, sweetheart."

At this point I realized I had four choices: buy the dress—only if we sold the family car; settle for something less—and endure the pathetic look of agony on my daughter's face for the next 50 years; use my VISA card—and view my eventual grandchildren behind prison bars; make the dress myself. Of course, there was a fifth—however ludicrous—option. Perhaps the person who designed the dress would feel compassion for my dilemma and out of the goodness of her heart just give me the dress? Naw! I was back to solution number four.

Three months later I found myself sitting cross-legged in the middle of the living room floor at 2:00 in the morning sewing tiny trans-

parent sequins onto volumes of Belgium satin and Venetian lace while the rest of the family slumbered in their beds. Sloshing about in my own self-pity, I mumbled something about being a victim of my own ill-advised choices. "There must be a lesson in this somewhere."

That's when I remembered reading about another wedding and another wedding garment. "But when the king came in to see the guests, he noticed a man there who was not wearing wedding clothes. 'Friend,' he asked, 'how did you get in here without wedding clothes?'" (Matt. 22:11, 12, NIV). While the garment in question was not that of the bride, it was a wedding garment nonetheless. I wondered about the man thrown out of the banquet hall for not being properly dressed, especially when Bible scholars point out that the king supplied the garments for his guests free of charge. Free—a gift! Solution number five.

I looked down at the crumple of lace and satin in my lap for a moment, and thought of the gracious King in the story—Jesus. In His hands is a garment of exquisite purity—my robe of righteousness. I recognize my need. I know what I want. I understand my options.

Like many throughout history, I could try to buy the garment. But the price tag of Calvary is too high. I could charge it—you know, pretending to myself and the world that I own the garment, while the bank of heaven holds the title. Or I could settle for a lesser quality garment. But both the King and I would know the difference.

Of course, I could make it, like I was doing with Kelli's gown. At this point the analogy falls apart faster than a poorly stitched hem. Because when it comes to my robe of righteousness, I've tried the do-it-yourself project for righteousness many times and failed. At least for me the seams are never straight and the stitches never come out even, no matter how carefully I follow the directions. Another option would be unthinkable: I could attend the wedding without a wedding garment, like the fool in the story—and find myself thrown into outer darkness.

Fortunately, my Jesus, a person of unmeasurable talents, has designed a robe of righteousness especially for me. It is guaranteed to fit perfectly, whether I wear size 2 or 22. Best of all, this custom-made wedding garment comes gift-wrapped in God's redeeming love. But I must accept it—and wear it. I must put complete trust in God's love.

Kay D. Rizzo

Saying Goodbye

For you know the grace of our Lord Jesus Christ,
that though he was rich, yet for your sake he became
poor, so that by his poverty you might become rich.
2 Cor. 8:9, RSV.

Breakfast sat in my stomach, hard and cold like the kitchen floor beneath my feet. I had to leave. It was too late now to change my mind.

It's only for a few days, I tried to console myself. But it was no use. I always felt this way before a business trip.

I moved into the warmth of the family room. As I settled on the couch, Mocha, one of our two keeshond puppies, snuggled across my feet. How soft her fur felt. And her hazel eyes, like pools of liquid trust, shone in the light of a single lamp. Her sister, Silver, lay nearby, fixing her gaze toward the corner of the forbidden bookshelves that she frequently chewed.

"Silvey," I whispered, "come here, girl." But she only stretched and yawned. Would Peter be able to practice obedience training with her while I was gone? She was going to need it! I'd have to discuss it with him on the way to the airport. Right now he was asleep.

I thought about him lying there—my favorite person. He said he'd miss me, of course, but he didn't mind my going too much.

I sighed. I really didn't want to leave any of this, not even for a few days. But as I rested my head against the back of the couch, the thought struck me: *What did Jesus leave behind when He made His trip to earth? Was there a favorite object in His Father's house that He loved to look at, to touch, to think about the history of?*

Maybe He had a pet. A favorite animal that He Himself created. Did He wonder how it would fare while He was gone for 33 years? How it would react when He returned?

What were His thoughts as He said goodbye to God? Did They hug and cry? Did They discuss what They would do in each other's absence? My mind staggered. *He who was verily God left behind all the glories of heaven to come to earth. He who traveled from star to star, from world to world, without the aid of mighty jets, traveled to earth*

in order to save us.

How could I possibly know what Christ left behind?

I questioned my own feelings about leaving home as I looked around the family room. The 100-year-old treadle organ sat along one wall, a solid-oak testament to a craftsman's faith from a time gone by. My mother's baby picture hung above it. And accenting the coffee table was a music box from my childhood.

What would I leave behind as my plane roared into the sky? Not much, I realized, as I felt Christ's love flow around me—a love that relinquished all the magnificence of heaven just so I could live there too. And what little I would miss would someday pale in the light of the most wonderful possession anyone could have, and never have to leave—our Lord and Saviour, Jesus Christ.   *Lyndelle Chiomenti*

Finding "Home"

Then I saw a new heaven and a new earth; for the first heaven and the first earth had passed away, and the sea was no more. Rev. 21:1, RSV.

I was flying six miles high and more than 500 miles per hour, going home after a two-week stay in my childhood home. I had just left home. Yet I was on my way home. Or was I? Where really is home?

The previous night I had snuggled down in "my" bed, in "my" room in the home my parents, brother, and I had moved into some 40-plus years earlier. It had been home until my Prince Charming had come and whisked me away to the life of a nomad (minister). Since then I had lived on the West Coast, Midwest, South, and now the East Coast.

This trip to my parents' home had not been a happy occasion. I had received sudden word that my father was dying. I left my East Coast home to fly to my West Coast home to be by Dad's bedside and to console Mom. There were days of little hope and days of possible hope as my gentle father tried valiantly to rouse from his un-

consciousness. He wasn't going to give up without a struggle. Our hearts would quicken as we held his hand and felt it feebly squeeze in response to our comments, or saw him weakly open his eyes and nod ever so slightly. A wiggle of his toe would delight us.

Long hours stretched into days, until it became apparent that his tired body could struggle no longer. He gave one long tired sigh and was gone. As my mother, brother, and I stood by his bedside with arms encircled and tears flowing, we knew home would never be the same again.

I returned to my present home, happy to be with my husband and willing to resume my duties. But home began to mean something different. I realized it could never really be here on this foreign planet. Though I have often longed to put my roots down deep, to live in one town and one home, I now know home is not in Washington, Texas, or Maryland. Everything here will always be temporary. Home is where my heavenly Father is.

I have lost my earthly father, but I have not lost my heavenly Father. He is preparing a permanent home for me where there will be no more moving, no more saying goodbye to a loved one. No more goodbyes at the airport, knowing Mom is going home to only a little black dog who can't understand why his master no longer sits in his favorite chair and holds him.

Yes, I definitely know now where home really is, and I'll never be fully satisfied until I get there!

Ellen Bresee

Live in the Lavender!

And be not conformed to this world: but be ye transformed by the renewing of your mind, that ye may prove what is that good, and acceptable, and perfect, will of God. Rom. 12:2, NIV.

It was Sabbath, and my husband and I were worshiping with our believers in the Crimea, just a short drive from the Black Sea. We had stayed at the church to greet our mem-

bers before coming to the pastor's house for a home-cooked Sabbath meal.

Now, after several courses of wonderful dishes, we pushed back from the table to try to catch our breath. I was always overwhelmed by the effort that my Ukrainian sisters put into a meal. I had taken note of the well in front of the house where the family drew their water to cook meals, bathe, and do the family wash. I remembered the rough dirt road that we had traveled to reach this home. Now I watched as the eldest son of the family sat quietly in the background. He was home for the weekend from a sanitarium; he had tuberculosis.

I sat quietly, trying to absorb my surroundings. The room was alive with the generous spirit of this family, but the hardships of their daily lives lurked in the shadows, including the pain of a bright young son with a crippling disease. No, life wasn't a "bed of roses" by any stretch of the imagination!

On either end of the food-laden table, rose-colored drapes flapped in the breeze. "What is that I smell?" I asked.

"Lavender," my host replied.

"It's wonderful!" I hastened to add.

In a flash the pastor's young daughter was up and out the back door. Moments later she returned with a handful of the sweetest smelling lavender I'd ever smelled. Over and over I held the blossoms up to drink in nature's perfume, while across the table from me the pastor's wife sat beaming. She was obviously pleased that they'd produced something that I was so enthused about. "Yes," she said with a broad smile, "we're so fortunate to live in a field of lavender!"

How her words tugged at my heart. I would remember her convincing smile long after I'd left the warmth of her home. I vowed that in the future, even when circumstances were less than perfect, I too would choose to live in a field of lavender!

Rose Otis

Be glad then, ye children of Zion,
and rejoice in the Lord your God.

Joel 2:23

Choosing Contentment

I have learned, in whatsoever state I am,
therewith to be content. Phil. 4:11.

I've struggled with the message of this text for many years, especially this past year. I've wanted to be content in my circumstances just as Paul says he felt content in his particular circumstances, but I must admit I'm still working on it. I haven't arrived as yet!

My husband does a lot of traveling, and I spend much time alone. I've moved frequently from country to country and city to city. I've had to make new friends, say goodbye to old ones, redecorate innumerable houses of all sizes and shapes, and try to find my way around new communities and neighborhoods.

I've wrestled with moving vans, boxes, barrels, crates, scratched furniture, and broken dishes, and adjusted to different congregations, schools, doctors, and well-meaning individuals who "just want to fill me in" on our new church or responsibilities. It's a real struggle to find contentment deep inside amid these changing circumstances. Contentment isn't always easy to achieve. There is a list of "if onlies" I rehearse from time to time. You know what I mean: "I would be content if only I could live somewhere else." Or "I would be content if only I could lose 10 pounds." And the list goes on.

However, when I read Philippians 4:11, I realize Paul is right. He learned that contentment is not dependent upon circumstances, that circumstances do not have to control us. He knew contentment is a state of mind, a gift of God, a *choice*. It comes with a deep, constant, and growing relationship with my Lord Jesus Christ. I can truly be content only by resting in Jesus, fully trusting Him to do what is best for me.

That's the kind of contentment I want, because I realize that contentment is not an option for the Christian. It is a must. It is only by having contentment and peace in my life that I can reflect His love and goodness to others.

God created a lovely, white, delicately sculptured shell to illustrate this idea to me. This shell has the lovely name of angel wing

because opened and laid flat, the two sides of this shell look like the wings of an angel. Where do you suppose this lovely shell lives? In the pure white sands of some tropical heaven? No! Does it move through the sea with speed and freedom, amazing all who gaze upon it? No! It lives elbow-deep in gray, gooey mud flats in Florida. In a lifetime it never sees the sky or the sun. It never leaves the hole that encases it. Only the determined shell enthusiast discovers and sees its delicate beauty.

To live, the angel wing must send a long, soft, flexible, soda straw-like siphon up through the mud into the water above. The tip of the siphon draws in food, and thus the angel wing thrives and builds its remarkable beauty. It doesn't complain or try to change its circumstances, but lives quietly and peaceably in the unusual place where the Creator placed it.

By God's grace I choose to be content in whatever location and circumstances my Creator places me. I want to be like the old Puritan who sat down to a scanty meal of bread and water. His contented heart cried out, "What? All this and Jesus Christ, too!"

Anita Folkenberg

Tell Me, Mary

"I am the Lord's servant," Mary answered. "May it be to me as you have said." Luke 1:38, NIV.

Sometimes during my personal devotions I wish I could bridge the gulf of time that separates me from the characters in biblical drama, especially the women who played such key roles in some of its cosmic scenes. Mary, for instance. If only I could talk to her, question her, what insights she could provide to my understanding of how it was to be a woman in her time.

Where did you find the courage, Mary, I would ask her, to accept the challenge of becoming the mother of a member of the Trinity?

You must have known, when you acceded to the plan announced by the angel, that you would be the focus of village gossip, of speculation and innuendo. Though honored above all women and innocent of the whispered accusations, you must have felt the weight of guilt imposed on you as you carried the divine burden in your womb.

How did you feel about your engagement to a man so much older than you, this widower, who, unless the Lord had intervened, would have put you aside? Had you been given any voice in the decision that espoused you to Joseph? Didn't the prospect of taking care of him and his home seem more than should be expected of someone of your tender age, scarcely yet a woman? Then before you were even used to the idea of mothering Joseph's children, were you not overwhelmed by the stupendous task of mothering *God's* child?

Whatever your fears, whatever feelings of inadequacy you may have had, you did not utter them. You only said, "Be it unto me," and magnified the Lord.

What an example you left me, left all of us women, Mary. When I am overwhelmed by a task the Lord has assigned me, I shall try to remember your submission.

I know the burdens of motherhood, of being teacher at school and teacher at home. I wonder how you found time to spend with that special Son, laying the groundwork for His unique mission of saving humankind and vindicating God's name. I wonder how you, who had no special training in behavioral sciences, were able to mediate between Him and His taunting stepbrothers. I see you at work—making the daily bread, *from scratch*; picking the stones out of the dry pottage-lentils; bargaining over the price of a jar of oil at the market; doing the washing at the village well; carrying the water jugs; spinning and weaving the family wardrobe; yes, even sweeping up the curls of planed wood and the sawdust in Joseph's shop because that was "woman's work."

I have known some pain in raising my family, have suffered for my children's pain. I still do. But you, Mary, knew the greatest pain of all—giving Him up, in your widowhood, to an unpaid, itinerant ministry and, ultimately, to the cross.

Tell me, Mary, the things you pondered in your heart, especially when that heart was pierced by the sword. Tell me how to bear up, Mary. I too would be a handmaid of the Lord.   *Jeanne Jordan*

Is It Over?

Even so it is not the will of your Father which is in heaven,
that one of these little ones should perish. Matt. 18:14.

My favorite weekends include a visit from our two grandchildren. While Heather still prefers to stay close to home, her 3-year-old brother, Ryan, is always eager to spend the night at our house.

He has a bedroom at our house that he calls his own, but lately he's become conveniently convinced that there are wolves in our upstairs. According to him, he's heard them growl, and he's even seen their *big* eyes! No amount of convincing has erased his fear of a night visit from the wolves. So we came up with the idea of using the mattress from the guest room crib to make him a bed on the floor beside Grandpa and Grandma's bed. Need I say that this was a very popular decision?

My husband and I had made up the "floor bed," and the three of us had knelt to pray that the wolves would be kept at bay through the night. We had showered Ryan with hugs and kisses and I had just tucked in his covers when I felt a little hand reach out for mine. "Let's hold hands, Grammie," he said. So we did.

It seemed that only a short time had passed when the next thing I knew there was some movement from the floor bed. I opened my eyes. Through streams of morning light creeping in around the shades, I saw Ryan watching me. He was kneeling on his bed, and his big blue eyes just cleared the top of our mattress. He asked me a simple question: "Is it over?" Now, in his mind that meant "Is the dull night over? That period of time when play ceases, and Grandpa lies still in his bed instead of playing hide-and-seek?" To a 3-year-old, nighttime is a dreadful waste of time, and when it's over—that's incredibly wonderful news! As for me, I can't remember a night that felt too long! But I couldn't help smiling at my grandson. "Yes, Ryan," I said. "It's over!"

Time is relative, isn't it? It all depends on our situation. For instance, our degree of tiredness or our age may determine whether or not we're ready for the night to be over. This same idea applies to

our spiritual life as well. Sometimes I feel like crying, "Lord, is it over?" Because I'm tired of the pain I see, and the separation, and the painful situations people get caught in in this world. But then there are other times when I want to plead just as urgently, "Lord, wait just a little longer!" That's when someone I love isn't walking with the Lord, or when I sense my own need to come closer to Him. There's only one Person we can trust to know when it's time for the "night" to be over, and that's our heavenly Father. Because when the timing seems just right for me, it may seem all wrong for you. He and He alone will know when there's been enough night. But for now, He's given us today to get ready for the glorious morning of His soon coming—when there will be no more night! Praise Him for His loving-kindness!

Rose Otis

The Diet

Oh, how I love your law! I meditate on it all day long. . . .
How sweet are your words to my taste, sweeter than
honey to my mouth! Ps. 119:97-103, NIV.

I would very much like to have a model figure. And although I've come to realize there is very little I can do about my height, I have tried many times to make some change in my width.

There was the grapefruit and cottage cheese diet, the "only fruit for supper" regime, the liquid diet, the no-fat program, and more. I lost weight on all of them for a while. The problem was that none of these diets was a lifestyle that was workable for very long.

Why am I telling you all this? It has to do with another diet, a spiritual diet. You see, I really want to be a beautiful, model Christian with faith, wisdom, and kindness showing in all I do. In my mind's eye the robe of Christ's righteousness fits me perfectly. But when I go to the mirror of God's love as shown in the Scriptures, I am appalled to find bulges and rolls in all the wrong places.

Now, I have tried many religious diets to take care of the prob-

lem. There was the diet of early-morning Bible study, the liquid course of fictional religious stories, and the self-denial method of fasting and praying. I was blessed by all these diets, but each method alone was too narrow to meet all my needs. At times I even tried the religious stress diet of letting my Bible fall open and reading everything I saw. The problem was that I couldn't hold out until the Lord came. He was taking too long for me to stick to one rigid plan. I'd begin to slip.

The answer I found is the same for my spiritual life as for my physical life. I don't need a quick-fix diet just to remove some bulges here and there. I need a complete lifestyle change that recognizes what it is my body and spirit need to be healthy and strong. I need a variety of foods all through the day to sustain me—hearty, healthy foods that taste wonderful and that I can chew on. I need exercise to keep my muscles and faith strong.

Now, knowing this doesn't mean always achieving the ideal. But I have finally been freed from the restless and unsuccessful search for a quick diet to get me into that perfect robe and hold me until the Lord comes. I now have a way of life that I can live with if the Lord comes today, tomorrow, or not until sometime long in the future.

And when I look in God's mirror, He says to me, "O taste and see that the Lord is good" (Ps. 34:8). And I say to Him, "Oh, how I love your law! I meditate on it all day long. . . . How sweet are Your words to my taste, sweeter than honey to my mouth!" This is a way of life that beats any diet I ever tried.   *Rachel I. Patterson*

Joy in the Lord

The joy of the Lord is your strength. Neh. 8:10.

I fell in love and got married in 1967 while the war in Vietnam was in full swing. My husband was a private in the U.S. Army, which meant moving far away from the support of my family. I had never lived in a military town, and had no idea what to expect.

The rent for our little cottage alone took 70 percent of my husband's monthly pay! The utilities, tithe, and enough groceries for *one week* took the rest! That left no money for gas, food for the other three weeks, clothing, entertainment, or anything else! Very few jobs were available for wives, and there were hundreds looking for those few jobs!

I had never lived in such poor conditions. It had been many, many years since those worn-out hardwood floors in our little cottage had seen any varnish or wax! The walls were dirty, so we bargained with the owner for some paint, which he agreed to purchase if we would do the painting ourselves. Of course, we first had to fashion scrapers to remove the old paint, which was so bad it was peeling and curled in some of the rooms. We shampooed the living room furniture in an effort to improve the appearance.

I had been raised in a good home in which my parents provided me with everything I needed and wanted. I had been pampered and spoiled. The reality of life was a shock, and needless to say, I was bored. I didn't have any friends, and our savings were evaporating quickly. I sat home alone day after day feeling sorry for myself, and I became more and more depressed as I took my eyes off Jesus and looked at myself.

My only comfort was my loving husband and the Lord. As my depression grew deeper, I became more and more angry with myself. I didn't like myself that way. I realized that my only help out of the depression was God.

I reached out to Him in prayer, confessed my sin, asked forgiveness, and pleaded for help in overcoming my self-pity and depression. I studied the Bible and read *The Desire of Ages*. I found today's scripture and this promise: "A merry heart doeth good like a medicine: but a broken spirit drieth the bones" (Prov. 17:22). I daily claimed these promises as my own. I began singing all the songs I could remember from Sabbath school, and borrowed a songbook from church and wrote down the words to more songs that I knew the tunes to.

I made a list of all my blessings and daily added to the list, although sometimes I had a hard time finding a blessing. As I focused my thoughts on God and His goodness to me, praised His name, and recognized and thanked Him for all the blessings I had, I gained the victory over self, and my whole outlook on life began to change. I

Therefore the redeemed of the Lord shall return,
and come with singing unto Zion; and everlasting
joy shall be upon their head:
they shall obtain gladness and joy... Isa. 51:11

learned through many repeated experiences to be happy wherever God put me.

Now, 25 years later, I can look back and thank God for the way He has led in my life. My husband became a minister, and we have had 18 wonderful years learning to depend daily on God, to be creative on a minister's income, ministering to others in crisis, and helping them to learn to be joyful and trust in God.

In retrospect I see that every experience He allowed me to go through was to teach me not to count this earth as my home and to prepare me to help others.

God's promises to us are sure. We need only to claim them as our own, determine to be happy regardless of our circumstances, and accept His grace to gain the victory.

Celia Cruz

The View from My Quarters

I will be glad in the Lord. Ps. 104:34.

A visitor to a small town asked an old resident, "What kind of town is this?" The visitor had a desire to move to the town. The old man replied by asking a question: "Well, what kind of town did you come from?"

The visitor proceeded to tell about the terrible town he had just left. The people did not act friendly, they felt that the churches contained hypocrites, and unemployment existed everywhere.

"You have just described this town, too," exclaimed the old man. "This town is just as bad."

Not long after, another visitor, thinking of moving to the same town, inquired about the town from the same old gentleman. The old man responded with the same question. "What kind of town did you come from?" The young visiting man described his last town as friendly. The people felt concerned for others, the churches acted

caring and exhibited strong spirituality. Plenty of jobs existed.

"That is wonderful!" exclaimed the old man. "And you will find this town is just like that. It is a wonderful place to live."

When I heard this story, I thought of how well it fits some people I have met. Believe it or not, when we lived in Hawaii, we met many people who were very unhappy there who found many things wrong with "paradise," while others were putting in for extensions. The same is true here, and it was in Missouri, and New York City, and everywhere we have been. Some love the weather, some hate it. Some love the church, and some stop attending. Some can't get the Sabbath off from their hospital unit, and the next Seventh-day Adventist in the same unit has no trouble. What is the difference? Attitude!

Most people keep the same attitude no matter where they live or work or worship. The location isn't nearly as large a determinant as is attitude.

What can you do if you find yourself in a location, church, or job that you don't like? First, decide to like it anyway. Then begin to find all the positive things you can about it. Make positive things happen. Don't wait for everything to happen to you. Determine to make the workplace more pleasant for those around you. Begin to look for things to do to improve the church—volunteer a little, and you will soon find plenty of things to do and wonderful people to work with. Try to make your community a better place just because you have been there. Be a good neighbor and reach out to the community as time allows.

There isn't much one can do about those endless miles that separate you from home, or the weather, or that inhuman boss, or even the pastor, but by taking a positive attitude and doing what you can do in a situation, you will soon find that you live in a great place with nice people and the best church around. Try it—you just might like it.

Maranatha!

Ardis Stenbakken

Give Until It Aches

Cast your bread upon the waters, for you will find it
after many days. Eccl. 11:1, RSV.

In the late seventies, when my husband was working in a check clearing bureau, an Adventist friend related a wonderful experience. Recently, he said, he was having financial problems, and was down to his last $100, with which he intended to pay his rent. So he went to the administrative offices to pay. On his way he met this poor, shabby-looking lady with a little child. She greeted him, then she cried and said, "My child and I are very hungry. We've been without food for several days."

He was stunned. He didn't know how to respond. He said to himself, "If I give this lady this money, my family and I are going to be thrown out of the house, because that's what the administration normally does when one cannot pay the rent. And if I don't give, the poor lady will go hungry again, and what will God say?" He then decided to give the whole $100 to the lady, who thanked him profusely.

When he got home his knees were wobbling. He did not tell his wife, he was so afraid. He kept on praying that he would not receive a letter from the administration until the end of the month. Such a letter never came. Immediately when he got his salary, he thanked God and went to pay his debt for the two months.

But the administrative clerk insisted that he had already paid his rent for the past month, this month, and the following month. They argued, but the clerk showed him copies of the receipts. He kept on saying, "There's a mistake somewhere," but the clerk was adamant. So he went home and praised the Lord.

Who do you think paid that rent? It is said that if you open your hand to give, the Lord puts back something in return. But if you close it and don't give, He has nowhere to put your blessings, because your hands are closed. So give to the poor; the Lord will refund you!

Lindeni Xaba

Through the Fire

But my God shall supply all your need according to his riches in glory by Christ Jesus. Phil. 4:19.

The sun shone warm and gentle on our garden that Sunday as we gathered a crop of string beans and tomatoes for the freezer. The bees hummed in the scented air as we took our bounty to the house.

My husband was church pastor, and our four children were healthy and intelligent. Our oldest daughter had just returned to academy for her second year. I should have been happy, but depression hung over me like a cloud. For months the struggle to make our small salary cover the needs of our growing family had distressed me. I had denied myself the option of employment outside the home, choosing rather to stay at home to nurture our preschool children. Did God understand? Could He supply our needs?

Suddenly there was a piercing scream from the basement! "Ron, quick—it's Kerry!" My mind raced as I thought of our 13-year-old son filling his tractor mower with gasoline in preparation for his day of mowing.

With heart pounding wildly I leapt down the basement steps to be confronted by a veritable wall of fire. Flames filled the entire garage area. I could see Kerry grab the fire extinguisher just as his father ran up behind him through the open garage door. At least he's moving! Was he hurt otherwise? Dashing back upstairs where smoke was already coming through the floor, I punched the operator button on the phone and yelled, "Fire! Fire!" and ran from the house with the only treasure saved—a telephone book!

Where were the younger children who had been playing in the back part of the house? Shelly, 7, hearing the commotion, followed me out of the house. Panic seized us as we saw, amid the swirling smoke, 4-year-old Robbie framed in the picture window. Hysterically I darted back for him just as he ran out the door. Smoke billowed from doors and windows as they popped in a series of quick explosions. Minutes seemed like hours till we heard the sirens of fire trucks. A crowd gathered quickly and someone

asked, "Is there anyone in the house?"

"No," I answered. "We are all here."

"You have all that's important" was the reply.

We found that Kerry was unhurt, only his hair singed and his hands superficially reddened. We knew this to be a miracle after we learned that a five-gallon can of gas had exploded in his hands.

Months later, as I thought of the experience—the almost total loss of our household possessions—I could see God's hand. I remembered the miracle of the $50 bill that had been anonymously given my husband several weeks before and that was found still intact though scorched around the edges amid the ashes on my husband's desk. This was used as a deposit to obtain temporary housing. God also preserved the food inside the severely damaged freezer. Things were restored in time, but the greatest restoration was my faith in God to supply our needs, and the realization that temporal things can vanish in an instant. The only important thing is life itself. Our lives had been spared, and in walking "through the fire" we had "not been burned" (Isa. 43:2).

Joan M. Neall

No Use Pretending

Be sure your sin will find you out. Num. 32:23.

Our family was enjoying a weekend holiday in Ootacamund, a resort area in the Nilgiri Hills of southern India. On Sunday morning we planned to eat masala dosai at a restaurant. We were about to leave our pet monkey, Bosco, in the hotel room when 12-year-old Stephen noticed a broken windowpane through which Bosco could escape. He would have to go with us.

However, at the hotel entrance a sign said "No pets allowed."

"Lock Bosco in the car," my husband ordered.

"He'll get out!" 8-year-old David protested. "He knows how to roll down the windows." A leash wasn't the answer either, for Bosco

knew how to untie knots and undo hooks.

"Mom, you'll have to baby-sit Bosco while we eat," 11-year-old Esther suggested. "We'll bring something back for you."

"Hey! That's no fair!" I complained. "I know what we can do. I'll hide him inside my sweater."

I buttoned the bulky knit red sweater all the way down the front and stuffed Bosco inside. Crossing both arms over my middle, I said triumphantly, "Now, there! Nobody will know we have a pet!"

Bosco began to squirm.

"Sssh! Bosco!" I warned. "Be a good monkey!"

Bosco did his best.

"OK, we're ready!" I whispered. "Let's go! Now walk in as though everything is normal."

Ron walked in first, followed by our three children. The only vacant table was on the far side of the room. Bosco smelled food and began clawing for an opening. I spread my hands and pressed him tighter against my stomach.

Suddenly all talking in the restaurant stopped. Everybody was staring at me! I looked down. There hung two feet of monkey tail right down the center of my skirt!

Just then Bosco popped a button and stuck his head out to see what was happening. Everyone burst out laughing! It was no use pretending any longer. I brought him out for all to see.

A waiter headed my way, and my embarrassed family tried to act as if they had never seen me before. Fortunately the gracious management let Bosco stay with us. Afterward I wondered why I had tried so hard to pretend he wasn't there.

Every once in a while I'm tempted to button up my sweater to hide my mistakes inside, hoping people will not discover what kind of person I really am. I think that if I can just cover my failings no one will know that I'm not really the super-perfect Christian I pretend to be. But sooner or later the tail of my sin slips out for everyone to see.

"Lord, help me today to stop pretending. Make me open and transparent, with nothing to hide."   *Dorothy Eaton Watts*

Transformation

You, O Lord, keep my lamp burning; my God turns my
darkness into light. Ps. 18:28, NIV.

His coveted box had finally arrived. It protected the material for a water lily Tiffany-style lampshade. Uroboros, the name of the glass that would fashion this shade, was supposed to be some of the most exquisite glass ever crafted. Surely, with such an exotic name, it would ripple with color. But when my husband opened the box, I found it difficult to mask my disappointment. The blues and greens for the water were muddy in tone and rough in texture. The only glass I could muster enthusiasm for were the pinks that would compose the water lilies. Because it was his hobby, I bit my tongue to prevent negative words from escaping my lips. But how could I remain silent when it came time to put the finished product where he wanted it—in the family room right next to where I usually sit? I decided, however, to worry about that dilemma later, for he predicted it would take six months to complete in his spare time.

During the next two months I was away from home. But I received weekly reports that always included an update on the shade. "Since you're not here, I'm really making great progress," one report went. Did that mean that he missed me, or that my usual presence hindered his creativity? I chose to believe the former. But my real concern was that he would finish sooner than he thought, and I would have to decide sooner than I thought what I would say about the shade's final resting place.

I am home now. And the last progress report I received solved my dilemma. It was Friday evening when I noticed an unusual glow in the dining room. As I entered the room, I blinked in disbelief. There on the table sat a lamp base, lighted and crowned with the Tiffany shade. The light had transformed the murky blues and greens into hues that shimmered like water. The lilies floated serenely (and somewhat smugly). After the shade is cleaned and polished it will glisten even more. And we will place it *across* from where I usually sit in the family room so I can look at it often.

But let all those that put their trust in thee rejoice:
let them ever shout for joy,
because thou defendest them: let them also that love
thy name be joyful in thee. Ps. 5:11

What a difference light made in the presentation of the glass. I now know that the thickness and folds of Uroboros glass are designed specifically to catch, hold, and reflect the light. Just as we are designed to reflect Christ in our lives. Without Him our lives are like the dark, lifeless glass as it first came from the box. Without Him our lives are muddy and rough. But when we invite Him to live in our hearts, His truth will transform us. His love will shine forth. And we will reflect the rainbow hues of mercy that surround His throne.

Lyndelle Chiomenti

A Tranquilizer for Problems

A cheerful heart is good medicine, but a crushed spirit dries up the bones. Prov. 17:22, NIV.

Most of us are overworked and underlaughed. Yet laughter is a wonderful tranquilizer for problems. Dr. Joyce Brothers writes that humor "lets us detach ourselves from our troubles, laugh at them, and eventually overcome them." She says that "studies indicate that those who lack a sense of humor are short on emotional stability, self-confidence, and the ability to endure stress. Those with a good sense of humor tend to be more resilient and are able to cope better." Medical research suggests that laughter may help reduce the risk of heart disease, high blood pressure, and stress-producing emotions.

Yes, a good belly laugh has been scientifically proven to react positively on our body systems. In his book *Laugh After Laugh*, Dr. Raymond Moody tells of a clown performing for seriously ill children in a hospital. One small girl giggled with delight as he approached. There was immediate excitement from the hospital staff. The clown learned that this child had been catatonic and unresponsive for months. Laughter became the breakthrough.

Norman Cousins, in *Anatomy of an Illness*, tells how he discovered the benefits of laughter in treating his own serious illness. After

watching funny television programs, such as *Candid Camera*, he experienced less pain. Ten minutes of mirthful laughter resulted in two hours of pain-free sleep.

Humor helps us keep the stresses of life in perspective. I believe humor is a matter of survival for stressed women. That's why I use lots of it in my seminars. Humor is a blessing.

One of my favorite stories is of the newly married wife who, after her shower, bounded into the living room—stark naked—to surprise her husband with a hug and a kiss. To her horror, he was not alone. The pastor had stopped by for a visit. With a shriek she fled into the bedroom. Other women might have found a new church home, but she marched up to her pastor the very next week and said, "Hi, I'm Jan. I wasn't sure you'd recognize me with my clothes on." Together they shared a good laugh, and the awkwardness passed.

If something doesn't go exactly the way you think it should today, try laughing about it rather than coming unglued. It will take the sting out of a situation and put a smile on your face.

And remember it's scriptural. Bildad encourages Job by saying, "He will yet fill your mouth with laughter and your lips with shouts of joy" (Job 8:21). And David describes a return to prosperity with the words "our mouths were filled with laughter, our tongues with songs of joy" (Ps. 126:2).

Someone has said, "If you are happy, notify your face." Good advice. Start today with a smile and take it from there.

Nancy Van Pelt

The Opposite of Love

My command is this: Love each other as I have loved you. Greater love has no one than this, that he lay down his life for his friends. John 15:12, 13, NIV.

"The opposite of love is not hate, it is indifference." The reminder hangs above my desk, jolting me a dozen times a day.

Peggy's nagging back pain is still hanging on today, I overhear her say as I walk by. I wonder if Pam's unsmiling face is a mark of suffering inside. Cynthia's adored and only granddaughter won't be out of the hospital for her first Christmas, the doctors have just announced to the agonizing family. Neighbor Lynne is going through a very painful divorce and now has two small children to parent and support on her own. Someone mentions that Lillian is unhappy in her new job.

"They will know you are Christians by your love." Having grown up in church, I've sung those words over a thousand times. But they never cease to haunt me, to make me feel uneasy, somehow negligent, inadequate, uncomfortable. Of course I love the world out there, I rationalize; I accepted Christ as my Saviour when I was only 10 years old and I've never wandered since. Surely through all these years the world has seen that I love it. Or has it?

Walking into Linda's kitchen one day, I was stopped short by something new on her refrigerator door. "Love is something you do." Immediately my mind protested. Something you do? I had always thought love was something you felt. Mulling that over for days afterward, I realized finally that it made sense, that it was indeed the gospel. In fact, this must be what Jesus meant when He commanded those first Christians, "Love each other as I have loved you," and in the same breath added, "Greater love has no one than this, that he lay down his life for his friends."

The words hang on, coming back each time my gaze falls on that scrap of paper above my desk. "The opposite of love is not hate; it is indifference." "Love is something you do." "Love as I have loved." The inner voice pushes at my complacency, my satisfaction with my life, and my level of Christlikeness. If you love Peggy, Pam, Cynthia, Lynne, and Lillian, I hear it say, *do something*. Show them you care about the hurts in their lives, the problems that seem too big to climb over, the pain that hangs on and on and on. Of course you are busy; so is everyone else, but doing needn't take much time. Maybe just a card, a deserved compliment, or a gentle hug will lift a tiny part of those clouds that hang over their worlds. Maybe you can do more. But do something, for doing nothing is the opposite of love.

Those words still hang above my desk and will for many months to come, I am sure. Each and every day I need to be reminded again

that love may not always involve feeling, but it always involves action. If I love, I will do.   *Carole Spalding Colburn*

Puppy Sins

Bow down Your ear to me, deliver me speedily; be my
rock of refuge, a fortress of defense to save me.
Ps. 31:2, NKJV.

Leaving our subdivision for my morning errands, I got stuck behind a school bus with its flashing red lights. Impatient to go on with my day, I twiddled my thumbs on the steering wheel of the car. That was when I noticed the reason for the extended delay. An adorable little puppy had been playing with the children waiting at the bus stop, and it insisted on going to school on the bus with the kids.

A little girl put her backpack and lunch down on the bus steps and picked up the puppy, carrying it back to the curb. Then she ran as fast as her little legs would carry her onto the bus. But right behind her was that stubborn little puppy. Again she picked up the puppy, carried it away from the bus, set it down, and hurriedly scrambled on board. But the little puppy was as fast as she was, and once again she picked it up to place it outside the school bus. This happened over and over—the girl setting the puppy on the curb, then running onto the bus with the puppy right on her tail.

Assuming this might take all day without some sort of intervention, I jumped out of my car and held the puppy until the bus with its flashing red lights had moved on down the road. I found the puppy's home and deposited it there before going into town.

As I drove off, errand list in mind, foot making up for lost time on the accelerator, God spoke. He compared the puppy on the curb to the pet sins in my life that follow me around. He reminded me that I need Someone bigger than myself to hold the sins back so I can continue on my spiritual journey. Not only does He give me power over those pet sins; He deposits them right where they

belong, in the depths of the sea. Are there any pet sins in your life that you'd like to turn over to Him?

Ronna Witzel and *Shonna Dalusong*

Making Papa Proud

He does not punish us as we deserve or repay us for our sins and wrongs. Ps. 103:10, TEV.

For nearly 20 years I deceived my father. I can admit it now and even laugh at myself for thinking the deception necessary. You see, I pretended to love spinach, when in truth I could barely gag it down even when disguised with butter or lemon juice. But Papa liked spinach, and I was determined to be like him. I was happiest at those times when my mother said that I was just like my father—usually, alas, just before I got in trouble for something!

Spinach was not the only thing I pretended to like—it was only my most successful attempt to be like Papa. After his offhand remarks during a softball game that I both ran and threw "like a girl," I strove mightily to swagger like the guys in the neighborhood and spent hours throwing a softball against the garage door to improve my aim. It didn't help. To this day I still run and throw like a girl!

I talked to my father about softball when I was an adult. To be more accurate, I apologized for my lack of skill and all my other wimpy traits, like collecting dolls. Basically, I apologized for not being the son I was sure he always wanted.

I used to spend a lot of time apologizing to God, too. Seeing Him as a father figure, I often tried the same tactics to earn His love. I performed good deeds whether or not my heart was in them, simply because I wanted to make Him proud. Like my earthly father, I saw Him as someone to be copied, so I tried to accomplish things I obviously wasn't suited for. I was so busy trying to be perfect that I had little time left for fun. Every childhood mistake was worried over as

I begged forgiveness from the Father I was trying to emulate.

Then came the revelation, not in a celestial vision, but in the simple acceptance that no matter how hard I tried I could never be more than a pale imitation of my Creator. All the while I thought I was trying to make Him proud, when I was really too full of my own pride to accept His gifts. I was too proud to accept someone else's help. I believed that I had to pay my way to heaven. It took me a long time to realize that Jesus Christ had already paid for my soul with His life and that, like Papa's love, it was not something I had to eat spinach for. I still try to make Him proud of me, but the guilt and the fear of failure are gone.

Even after my confession, Papa never admitted to wanting a son. He insisted that daughters were far superior, and that he never cared much for sports anyway. Of course, maybe by telling me that, he was just paying me back for all that spinach I ate.

Gina Lee

God's Care

Consider the ravens: for they neither sow nor reap;
which neither have storehouse nor barn;
and God feedeth them: how much more are ye better
than the fowls? Luke 12:24.

In January of 1991 war in the Persian Gulf began, and the United States sent thousands of American men and women to the area. I had never seen my country in a major conflict; war was something from a history class—events with dates and places to memorize. So I followed the news diligently, read newspaper clippings, and engaged in lively discussions with friends over dinner.

Then, with a phone call in the wee hours of the morning, the word "war," and the horror and pain it causes, took on new meaning for me: my sister was leaving for Saudi, leaving her husband and 3-year-old daughter behind. Suddenly I followed the updates with more intensity, straining to hear if there had been any casualties. I

wrote postcards with texts on them every day. And I prayed for her safety like never before.

I imagined my sister with scud missiles whizzing overhead, dust stinging her nose and eyes, and homesickness hanging over her like a shroud.

One day I listened with fear as the radio announcer stated that three American personnel had been killed in practice drills. I shivered at the thought that one of them could be my sister. I quickly shared this news with a friend and was shocked at her response. "It's only three," she shrugged. "That's not that many." When I imagined my sister fighting in the desert, and how the families of the three who were killed must be feeling, I whispered, "If it's someone you love, it's one too many."

Later I thought about that statement, and realized anew how special each one of us is to God. There are so many people on earth, it's hard to imagine that God really knows us individually and cares what happens to us. Yet God says that He knows how many hairs are on our heads, and that our names are written on the palms of Jesus' hands. He will never force us to know Him; yet He yearns for each one of us to choose Him and share His friendship. God longs for us to find the peace and joy that can be ours by following Him, and gently woos our hearts to choose eternity in heaven with Him. Though the world may consider one or two lives a small loss, when God considers losing us, He says, "Even one of My precious children lost is one too many."

Kathryn M. Gordon

Why Not Ask for More?

Until now you have not asked for anything in my name.
Ask and you will receive, and your joy will be complete.
John 16:24, NIV.

He was a modern prodigal, so the story goes. Like the prodigal of the New Testament (Luke 15), he too had spent the fortune his father had given to

Rejoice evermore.

1 Thes. 5:16

him—and was now one of the homeless, finding his food wherever he could. One day he received word that his father had died. As he walked along the street, thinking about it, he wondered if his father's will would permit him to have just $5 so he could have one good meal. The thought made him quicken his steps, and he hitchhiked back to his hometown.

Arriving in town, the son located the address of the legal firm that had taken care of his father's business and went to the attorney's office. Two of the lawyers were visiting as he entered. When they offered their help the son said, "Is there anything in my father's will that would permit you to give me $5 so I can have one good meal?" One attorney gave an affirmative answer and handed him $5. The man happily left the office, anticipating all of the good things he was going to eat.

After the door to the office closed, the attorney who had answered said to the other, "What a pity! His father's will reads, 'Give my son any amount that he asks for.'"

Whenever I think about this story, I always wonder if this is why so many of us go through life with so little of God's love in our hearts; why we have so few answers to prayer; why we claim so few of God's promises.

We must learn to ask! There is no need to go through each day of life metaphorically with just $5, when we could have $5 million. Are we not the children of God (1 John 3:1, NIV)? God tells His sons and daughters to "ask"!

Remember that our Father's will reads: "Give My child any amount that he or she asks for." Oh, let us ask—and receive.

Alice Smith

The Key

Judge not, that ye be not judged. Matt. 7:1.

I struggled with a document in my computer. There seemed to be no rhyme or reason why the words on that page would not line up or move to the position where I wanted them. Keystrokes and commands that normally would have resulted in predictable behavior now only produced chaos. Computers may not have "real" brains, but at times they do seem to have minds of their own.

I was at the point of exasperation when I remembered a neat little command in my machine called "reveal codes." This wonderful little key opens up a window on the screen that reveals all the codes that have been placed in a document. Understanding what behavior each code produces, you are enabled to reason from cause to effect and subsequently remedy the situation. After searching through my document, I discovered a misplaced and unwanted code to be the culprit, and its removal through my "delete" key solved all my problems.

Have you ever known people who were obstinate or unpredictable? Were you ever exasperated because they would not act or react the way you thought they should? Most of us have "codes" in our brains that cause us to act in certain ways. And most likely we are not even aware of the presence of those codes. Maybe their entrance into our subconscious stems back to a childhood situation. Perhaps they were implanted through the subtlety of the media. Or we may have even consciously implanted an obnoxious code or two in our minds on purpose.

So we must realize that people react to situations according to how they have been "coded" or programmed. Wouldn't it be nice if we had access to a "reveal codes" key so that we could peek into their brains and see what makes them tick? Reasoning from cause to effect, perhaps we would be more understanding and tolerant. Perhaps we would express more love and understanding instead of criticism.

But because we don't have a "reveal codes" key, we don't have access to all the facts, and that's exactly the reason that God tells us to "judge not." Only God has access to that key. Only He knows why

we act the way we do, and therefore only He can be a true Judge.

So whenever we're tempted to judge the actions of our husband or children or that obnoxious coworker, let's remember "the key." Then we can ask God for help to look beyond the obvious and see the person the way God sees him or her, and loves them anyway!

Nancy Cachero Vasquez

As a Little Child

Except ye be converted, and become as little children, ye shall not enter into the kingdom of heaven. Matt. 18:3.

My older children were born in the 1930s while we still suffered the effects of the Great Depression. Our farm life provided food, but money for clothes and other "extras" was practically nonexistent. And little boys grow! With springtime they could discard their winter coats but still needed a light wrap. Mickey's one sweater barely covered his elbows or his tummy. Worn for play, it became stained and torn.

The Saturday night trip to town was an important event for most farmers. Mickey liked to walk through the stores and look at all the pretty things. But on this particular night, he stayed in the car with Daddy and baby brother while I searched for a sweater in the few stores our small town provided. I found a pile of them, but the $1.10 they cost was more than our strained budget would stand. Sadly, I returned to the car and told Mickey that we'd have to wait until next week. His patient acceptance hurt me more than a violent protest would have.

The next week proved to be financially more stringent yet. Again I had to tell him we must wait. Bravely he swallowed his disappointment, saying that Jesus would help us.

As I listened to his confident prayers, I inwardly determined he would get his sweater if we didn't eat next week. But as we started for town the next Saturday night my husband told me, "You'll have to cut the groceries to the bone tonight. I had to buy a part for the car."

All the way into town Mickey chattered about the sweater Jesus would give him. I tried to bolster my faith by his, but there was no way I could squeeze $1.10 from our small grocery allotment. "Please, Lord," I prayed. "I don't know how, but honor this little boy's faith. He trusts You."

With not the slightest idea of what my procedure would be, I strode purposefully to the department store. I found the same pile of sweaters. But lying on top was a pretty, fuzzy blue one marked 29 cents. All the rest were $1.10.

I could hardly believe it. Shakily I asked a clerk, "Is there some mistake?"

She smiled brightly. "That sweater was left over from last year, found in the stockroom yesterday. These others are part wool. This one is brushed cotton, but it is very warm."

I carefully counted out the coins and hurried to the car.

Naturally, it fit perfectly. It was made by angels. Mickey happily wore it as he looked at the pretty things in the store. Some folks smiled at the boy in the fuzzy, blue sweater—just the color of his shining eyes. A few may have noticed that his mother's eyes were shining too.

Lillian Lawrence

A Light in the Night

You are all [daughters of the light] and [daughters] of the day. We do not belong to the night or to the darkness. So then, let us not be like others who are asleep, but let us be alert and self-controlled. 1 Thess. 5:5, 6, NIV.

John tossed his notebook and the hotel credit card room key he'd been issued on the bureau. It had been a long day. His brain swirled with all the new and exciting things he'd learned during the first day of meetings at the ministerial seminar. He glanced at the television and video menu card and shook his head. All he wanted was a hot shower and a good night's sleep.

The young pastor finished his shower. Wrapped in a hotel towel, he placed a call to the desk clerk asking to be awakened by 6:00. He took out his Bible and read a few favorite verses, then tossed the towel onto an easy chair and reached for the light switch beside the bed. But before turning off the light, he decided to leave on the bathroom light and close the door. Then if he awakened in the night, he wouldn't be quite so disoriented in a strange room.

Some time later John awakened with a terrible thirst. Drugged with sleep, he climbed out of bed. *Where am I?* he wondered. He scratched his beard. Then spotting the light shining beneath the door, he remembered. "Seminar, San Francisco, hotel . . ."

John groped his way toward the strip of light, opened the door, and stepped into the light. Before his eyes could adjust to the blinding glare, he heard the firm, gentle click of a lock. He glanced about in horror—suddenly wide awake. He was standing, towelless, in the empty hallway of the elegant San Francisco hotel. John had followed the wrong light.

Hearing the "bing" of the elevator and the sound of laughing female voices, he ripped the tablecloth from a nearby occasional table and wrapped it around himself before three middle-aged women turned the corner and walked toward him.

Wearing only his best smile and the purloined cloth, the preacher asked one of the women if she would please call down to the front desk on her room phone and ask that someone from room service be sent upstairs to unlock his door. He didn't try to explain his condition, nor did anyone ask. During the rest of the convention, the mortified man dodged meeting the three women face-to-face again.

Embarrassing? Yes, but hardly life-threatening. However, when it comes to spiritual light, the damage can be eternal. Ministries abound, each claiming to have new light. Cassettes, videos, films, books, pamphlets, and lecture series promote new discoveries on everything from the origin of man to the apocalypse and beyond. How can I know which light to follow?

Like John, the beams of light seeping under the closed doors can be confusing. It can send me in the wrong direction. Like John, the darkness can lull me to sleep. And when I awake, I will be disoriented. One stream of light can look much like any other until the end of our journey and the "door" clicks shut. Then it could be too late

to retrace my steps back to the place where I first lost sight of the true light. Chilling, isn't it?

It would be except that I serve a loving Saviour, the source of true light. He does not leave me to wander after every foolish fable that comes along. He's given me all the light I need in order to reach my destination of life eternal with Him. By keeping my eyes focused on Jesus and by claiming the promises of His Word, I will not stumble in darkness. With the guidance of Jesus' equal, the Holy Spirit, I will not become disoriented from sleep. I will discern the light of truth from error.

Jesus Himself said, "I am the light of the world. Whoever follows me will never walk in darkness, but will have the light of life" (John 8:12, NIV).

Kay D. Rizzo

That Missing "J" Key

I have come that they may have life, and that they may have it more abundantly. John 10:10, NKJV.

The *j* key on my typewriter doesn't work. It hasn't for three or four years. At first it was difficult. I would press the *j* key as I typed along, forgetting that it didn't work, and only later, as I proofread the page, would I discover the blank spots where the j's should have been. It was something of a strain to think of synonyms for all words with a j I was unable to use because of the broken key. But with time I learned to compensate quite well. "Envious" for "jealous," "happiness" instead of "joy," "trip" for "journey," etc. It really wasn't too difficult. In fact, after some time had passed I forgot there was a j key. I had trained myself to avoid the use of j words for so long that I would automatically use their synonyms. The j words just weren't part of my vocabulary any longer. I didn't need them. I had substitutes that worked quite well, and I doubt that anyone even noticed.

As I look at how I've replaced the *j* key on my typewriter by using similar words for the ones I'd really like to use but can't, I won-

der if I've done the same thing with the most important *j* word of all—Jesus? Do I find perfectly acceptable substitutes to take the place of a relationship with Him? Do I get so busy with my job, family obligations, and church involvement that I don't even notice that the place "J"esus wants to occupy in my life has been filled with a substitute? "Lord, make me always mindful of my *j* key—the only real key to an abundant life."

Joni Bell

Groomed for Service

*You say, "I am rich; I have acquired wealth and do not
need a thing." But you do not realize that you are
wretched, pitiful, poor, blind and naked. I counsel you
to buy from me gold refined in the fire, so you can
become rich; and white clothes to wear, so you can
cover your shameful nakedness; and salve to put on
your eyes, so you can see. Those whom I love
I rebuke and discipline. So be earnest and repent.
Rev. 3:17-19, NIV.*

My 6-year-old grandson and I were driving home after a day at White Water Park. Mulling over the great events of our special day together, he reached over, patted my arm, and said, "Grandma, I really do love you."

"I'm glad, Scottie."

"In fact," he added, "I love every part of you."

"Is that so, dear?" I asked.

"And you know the part I like best?"

"Tell me."

"I like your floppy muscles that jiggle when you move your arm."

Now, that's acceptance! That's the dimension of love that looks beyond the wrinkles, the trifocals, the floppy arms. Maybe grandmas are supposed to look like that. In any event, Scottie is satisfied.

Is this somewhat like God? Does God accept me just the way I am,

Rejoice in the Lord alway:
and again I say, Rejoice.

Phil. 4:4

wrinkles and all? In the physical world, yes, God accepts me. If I've done the best with what I have, perhaps He gives me a passing grade.

What about the spiritual world? I believe that in my spiritual life God accepts me just the way I am too. He sees the dimness of my spiritual eyesight. He notes the wrinkles of harmful habits. Surely He recognizes the spiritual tone to muscles that are prone to temptation. Like Scottie, God loves me just the way I am, but unlike Scottie, He loves me too much to leave me that way.

God wants to give me a strong, steady step to go on His errands, to walk confidently in His paths. He is both able and willing to strengthen my spiritual perception so that I can see the beauty of His character, enabling me to reflect it to others more clearly. He is eager to firm up my spiritual muscles to resist evil, developing power that Satan cannot match. My Father wants to condition me for heaven, in the meantime grooming me for fuller service while I am here on earth. He longs to make me a whole, beautiful person. He loves me far too much just to leave me as I am.

Lorabel Hersch

Good News

And the angel said to them, "Do not be afraid; for behold, I bring you good news of a great joy which shall be for all the people; for today in the city of David there has been born for you a Savior, who is Christ the Lord." Luke 2:10, 11, NASB.

Before the birth of our daughter I meticulously made out two lists of people who should be notified after her arrival. I gave one list to my mother, who would be at the birth, and I gave the other list to my husband. On my husband's list I had included the names of several of our close friends who waited fervently with us for the "overdue" entrance of our child. "Should the baby arrive in the middle of the night," I carefully explained to Curtis, "wait until morning to call these people." My sister, who had given birth to her daughter only a short time before,

had called us at 12:30 a.m. with the news of the birth, and I found it impossible to return to sleep. Birth is an exciting event!

Not surprisingly, Kimmy arrived at 1:39 a.m. on a Sunday morning. Exhausted from labor, I fell into a deep sleep at about 2:00 a.m. My husband and my mother, I assumed, went home and also fell asleep. It was not until several weeks later that I discovered the true course of events. A friend, whose name was on my husband's list, told me laughingly that he had received the good news at 2:30 a.m.! Shocked by this, I stared in disbelief at my husband. As if to answer my look of amazement he calmly replied, "With such good news, how did you expect me to go home and sleep?"

Although my husband had two other children, he was still so excited by the birth of our daughter that he had come home and called every person on his list at 2:30 in the morning! Rising to my husband's defense, our friend confessed, "After Curtis called me, I called the unit [the hospital ward where he and I both worked evening shift] so they could announce it at the morning meeting!" Good news is meant to be shared!

When God sent His only Son to this world, He also could not contain His joy. The angels sang out the message. Jesus Christ has arrived! Now, that was good news!

Is the precious message of Jesus Christ exciting to you today? Jesus came for each one of us; it is the most breathtaking birth in history. "For God so loved the world, that he gave his only begotten Son, that whosoever believeth in him should not perish, but have everlasting life" (John 3:16). Call someone today and share the precious news of Jesus.

Carel Clay

MORE *F*AMILY READING

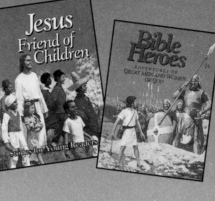

**God's Answers
to Your Questions**
You ask the
questions; it points
you to Bible texts
with the answers

**He Taught
Love**
The true meaning
hidden within the
parables of Jesus

**Jesus, Friend
of Children**
Favorite
chapters from
The Bible Story

Bible Heroes
A selection
of the most
exciting adven-
tures from
The Bible Story

The Storybook
Excerpts from
Uncle Arthur's
Bedtime Stories

My Friend Jesus
Stories for
preschoolers from
the life of Christ,
with activity pages

**Quick and Easy
Cooking**
Plans for complete,
healthful meals

**Fabulous Food for
Family and
Friends**
Complete menus
perfect for
entertaining

**Choices:
Quick and
Healthy
Cooking**
Healthy meal
plans you can
make in a hurry

**More Choices
for a Healthy,
Low-Fat You**
All-natural meals
you can make in
30 minutes

**Tasty Vegan
Delights**
Exceptional
recipes without
animal fats or
dairy products

**Fun With
Kids in the Kitchen
Cookbook**
Let your kids help
with these healthy
recipes

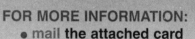

Health Power
Choices you can make
that will revolutionize
your health

Secret Keys
Character-building
stories for
children

Winning
Gives teens
good reasons to
be drug-free

FOR MORE INFORMATION:
- mail the attached card
- or write
  Home Health Education Service
  P.O. Box 1119
  Hagerstown, MD 21741
- or visit www.thebiblestory.com